Cutting the Strings

A Memoir

CAROLE LITTLE

ISBN-13: 978-0-9857004-0-9

DEDICATION

To my family for their support and encouragement throughout this process. I am truly grateful for their never-ending belief in me.

CUTTING THE STRINGS

ACKNOWLEDGMENTS

Special thanks to all those who supported me on the journey thus far. Many thanks to Jeannette Walls for encouraging me to embark upon the experience of a lifetime. Thank you Jane for being a wonderful audience and a great memoir buddy. Finally, to my writing coach, Max Regan, whose gentle coaching and sage wisdom guided me through this fabulous process.

"The world will continue to define you,

until you define yourself to the world."

—Unknown

Sai Sin

The Buddhist practice of *Sai Sin* is used in the north and northeast of Thailand for different ritualistic purposes. In one instance, before departing on a journey, attendants tie white threads onto the traveler's wrists during the ceremony. The individual is wished a safe journey, good luck, and good health. The white thread is believed to ward off evil spirits. The strings must be worn until they fall off or risk bad luck.

CUTTING THE STRINGS

PROLOGUE

One morning, as I was leaving my office, my cell phone started to ring. The Massachusetts number flashing on the screen was unfamiliar to me and I was surprised to hear the familiar female voice on the other end saying,

"Yes, I'm having software problems, and I need desktop support."

Just to be sure, I was hearing her correctly, I said,

"Excuse me?"

The voice that only an offspring will always recognize coming from the other end repeated her request for help with a software problem. I realized my mother must have a new cell phone number, which is why the number was unfamiliar to me. It had been more than four years since we had last spoken, but since it was obvious she had me listed on her speed dial, I knew it was by choice. How is it that a mother and her first-born daughter reach this point? In that moment, a lifetime of memories washed over me.

Chapter 1

My favorite show when I was six years old was *Boston Movie Time*. I loved any movie with Lauren Bacall, Humphrey Bogart, or James Cagney. The host of the show in 1962 was Frank Avruch, who started his career playing Bozo the Clown. When the show came on, you could always find me sitting in my mini Boston rocker in front of a black and white Motorola TV, completely mesmerized by the plot unfolding before me.

One night after dinner while I was totally engrossed in my movie, my mother stuck her head in the living room doorway and said, "Carole!" She must have called me several times before I heard her because she looked annoyed. "I need you to keep an ear out for your brother while I go out for a little bit. He's in the crib asleep. Okay?"

I nodded then turned back to the screen not wanting to miss the action unfolding. Since my stepdad, Charlie, had moved out, my mother seemed to be going out more these days.

Just as the movie ended, I became aware of a loud noise coming from the other side of the kitchen where my brother's bedroom was located. I decided to get up and investigate. As I went through the kitchen, it was obvious that the noise was coming from my brother Bob's room. I thought he was asleep, but the noise grew louder and louder and when I opened the door, I was shocked. Bob was in his crib, naked and was rocking back and forth so hard; he had moved his crib across the hard wood floor to the window.

Once I turned the light on, I couldn't believe my eyes. "Oh, my goodness! What have you done?" Bob had emptied his full diaper everywhere, including the pretty sheers that hung from the window! As I looked around the room to survey the damage, I could feel a knot growing in my stomach. He must have been awake for quite a while because he had time to maneuver his crib close enough to the wall to peel off a huge area of the brand new wallpaper.

I ran to get soap and water and a washcloth to clean Bob. Then I dressed him in a clean set of pajamas and sat him down on the scatter rug in the room while I cleaned up the rest of the mess. My mind was racing. How long had he been awake? Why didn't I hear him? My mother was going to be furious. I ran out of paper towels and turned to go for more when I noticed that somehow Bob had gotten a hold of my mother's red nail polish and was busy painting the hardwood floor with it. I needed to put this little guy in a place where he couldn't hurt himself or make any more messes. I looked at the walk-in closet and thought, "That's as good a place as any." I turned on the light, put Bob's blanket on the floor with some toys and sat him down in the middle of it. I closed the door to keep him out of harm's way.

It seemed to take forever, and when I got to the nail polish, it was dry. So I decided the best thing to do was cover it up with the scatter rug and hope she didn't notice. I couldn't do anything about the wallpaper so I'd just have to take the heat for that. I put a clean sheet on Bob's crib and took the dirty one along with his soiled pajamas out to the laundry room to place them in the washer. I went back to the room one last time to make sure I had cleaned everything up. Satisfied, I turned off the light and went back to the living room to watch *Mister Ed*. I loved that talking horse.

The show was almost halfway through when I heard my mother come through the back door. The next thing I knew, she was yelling, "Carole Jane! Where's your brother?" The minute she said it, I realized what I had done. I ran to Bob's bedroom, yanked open the closet door, and there was Bob, fast asleep on the blanket surrounded by his toys.

Chapter 2

My mother's cars typically never cost more than a few hundred dollars, which inevitably meant they did not last very long. I remember riding down the highway once and the top blew right off. I held onto my brother as tight as I could all the way home. My mother thought it was funny and told everyone about the scared looks on our faces. After that incident, I was glad the bus was our main form of transportation.

I loved it when we rode the bus downtown. The hustle and bustle of Main Street was so exciting. We would shop at Woolworth's, Kresge's, J. J. Newberry's, Filene's, and Denholm's Department Store. They were all located across from City Hall in the middle of Main Street. I cherished going downtown because it was alive with activity moving in all directions. People were getting off buses to go to work, conduct business, or shop while others were connecting to go to other parts of the city, and still others were going back home. The Paris Cinema was downtown too, and was often a great way to spend a Saturday afternoon.

My most memorable bus trip occurred when I was seven years old. My mom asked, "How would you like to take your brother, Bobby, on the bus to the movies?"

I couldn't believe my ears. "The movie theater downtown? Who will take us there?"

Taking a puff of her Benson & Hedges, she turned toward me. "You can both ride the bus."

Now this really piqued my curiosity. "Alone?" Before she could change her mind I said,

"Okay! When?"

Getting up out of the rocker she said, "Let's go and get you both ready."

After placing several coins into a piece of notebook paper, then folding it several times, my mother tucked it into my pocket, saying, "This is to get into the movies and for the bus ride home. The bus will drop you off and pick you up in front of the cinema. When you get out of the movies, look for the Upsala Street bus. Got it?"

In a very grown up voice, I answered, "I can read, Mom."

My mother walked us to Providence Street, where the bus usually parked since that was the end of the line for the Upsala Street bus. We boarded the bus and I put the money in the money box for both of us. My brother was only three years old and couldn't reach the hole to drop the money in.

"We're going to the matinee at the Paris." I proudly told the driver.

Smiling, he assured me, "We'll make sure you get off right in front, young lady."

We sat right in the first seat that faced forward on the right side of the bus so we could wave good-bye to our mother. We also got a bird's-eye view of the people getting on the bus. I liked scanning their faces and would smile at them as we made eye contact to see if they would smile back. There was a little old lady with a cane who sat across from us. Then there was a man with a stinky cigar hanging out of his mouth. He was bald, with a big belly and had a hard time walking toward the back as the bus pulled away from the curb. I thought he might fall on Bob, but at the last minute he grabbed onto the steel bar hanging from the roof of the bus to steady himself.

It was fascinating to watch the driver make change from the shiny coin holder hanging on the dash to the right of the steering wheel, and I loved watching the coins disappear from the bottom of the box when the driver pulled the lever. I marveled at the way the doors would magically open once the bus stopped, then close again just before the bus started up again. How did he make that happen?

It was a little more than two miles to downtown from where we boarded the bus in front of a big school. The bus would turn down a different street every so often and after about a mile or so, people would tug on the rope above the windows to make the buzzer sound to let the driver know they wanted to get off at the next stop. That was another reason we sat in the first seat: we couldn't reach the rope. It was about a twenty-minute ride with all the stops, but it seemed like an eternity to me. Finally, we pulled up in front of the cinema and I took my brother Bobby's hand.

"Come on, Bob. We're here."

Bob's little legs took the stairs one at a time so I waited on each step below him to make sure he didn't fall. Once we were on the sidewalk, we turned and waived to the bus driver who said, "Have fun you two," as he closed the doors and pulled away from the curb.

Holding Bob's hand, I walked up to the ticket window and pulled out two quarters to slide through the opening at the bottom of the glass. The woman behind the counter ripped off two tickets and slid them back toward me. We made our way into the theater, which was built in 1926. Formerly known as the Capitol Theatre, it had a rich history. The lobby was impressive with blue ornate molding along the walls and ceiling. As we walked on the dark red patterned plush carpet, we gazed at all the movie posters lining the walls of the historic lobby. We were guided by the plush red velvet ropes hanging from polished brass stands that lead to the two sets of mahogany doors that opened to either side of the theater. On the opposite side of the lobby was the concession counter, and the smell of hot buttered popcorn filled the air. Of course, we had to have some.

"How much is the popcorn, Mister?" I asked hoping it was within our budget.

"Ten cents a box," he replied in a matter of fact tone.

I reached into my pocket and had a dime. Back then there was only one size, which was just enough for us to share a box. With our popcorn in one hand and Bob's tiny hand in the other, I led him down to the front row to make sure we got a good view. The velvet curtains were still closed, but a man was playing the organ and the footlights lit up the stage in anticipation of the show. Bob and I munched on our popcorn while we waited. In no time the cartoons began. We must have been there all afternoon because when the screen finally went blank and we followed everyone out to the sidewalk, it was dark outside. I put my hand in my pocket one last time to pull out two quarters and two nickels to ride the bus back home and for some reason, I only had two quarters.

With panic starting to set in, I let go of Bob's hand so I could check my other pocket for the two nickels. I pulled the pocket lining all the way out just to make sure they weren't stuck and realized in that moment that two nickels were the same as a dime. When it occurred to me what I had done, I started to cry, which made Bob start to cry too. Through my tears, I realized a man was standing in front of us.

"What's wrong little girl?" His voice seemed kind and his face showed genuine concern.

"I only have two quarters left to get home and we need two more nickels to get on the bus."

The man reached into his pocket and pulled out a hand full of change. Picking out two shiny nickels and handing them to me, he said, "Here you go. Will this help you get home?"

Wiping my tears, I flashed back a huge smile and said, "Yes, Sir! Thank you very much!"

The familiar landmarks on the ride back home along with the routine of the driver and the rhythmic swaying of the bus in motion went a long way in calming the panic I had felt. By the time the bus reached the end of the line, the crisis had all but been forgotten. As I held Bob's hand on the walk back to our apartment, I was grateful for the kindness of strangers and decided there was no need to alarm my mother with the details.

Chapter 3

Just as my own world was transitioning and becoming unstable that year, so it would for the rest of America. A few short months after the trip to the movies, I recall the phone ringing and my Grandma Helen's voice on the other end saying,

"Tell your mother to turn on the TV. President Kennedy's been shot!"

For days, we were glued to the television, the sadness was overwhelming and somehow, even at the age of seven, I knew the goodness in my world was gone and that things would never be the same.

A few months later I woke up from a deep sleep to the sound of angry voices on the porch right outside my third floor bedroom window. It must have been sometime after midnight because I went to bed right after watching *Alfred Hitchcock Presents* just before midnight. The angry voices hurling slurred profanities belonged to my mother and her live-in boyfriend, Paul, who had obviously returned from a night of making the rounds at the local bars.

As I lay there listening, the voices became louder, and I tried to make sense out of the argument when Paul shouted, "I know Charlie is not Bobby's father!" Paul's voice got even louder. "You're a liar! Nothing but a damn liar! I saw how you and Duane looked at each other when you thought I wasn't looking. Do you think I'm that stupid?"

"You don't know what you're talking about!" My mother angrily insisted, "And I'll prove to you how wrong you are!"

I heard my mother storm past my bedroom door into my brother's room. Then she quickly returned to the third floor porch and threatened, "I'll throw this kid over the railing to prove I am telling the truth."

Paul shouted back, "You're out of your mind!"

She yelled back, "I *will* throw this kid off this porch! Are you going to take my word for it?"

As I lay there frozen, I could hear my heart pounding in my ears. Would she really do that? Was she really going to do that to my little brother Bob?

Life with my mother had become extremely unpredictable since my stepfather, Charlie, had moved out. In fact, I don't ever remember hearing my mother swear or see her drink before she decided to leave my stepfather. A few short months ago, right up until my seventh birthday, we were living in a quiet, three-decker house on Esther Street in a typical working class neighborhood that reflected life in Worcester, Massachusetts, during the early 1960s. Our three-bedroom apartment located on the first floor had an eat-in kitchen, a living room and a parlor. It was a step up from the one bedroom apartment on Buffum Street, where we had lived previously, after my mother married Charlie.

Our landlord, Mr. Wiscniewski, his wife, and three children lived above us on the second floor, while the people on the top floor were the typical American melting pot mix of English, Irish, French, and a smattering of something else. I always had friends to play with outside. We belonged to the neighborhood, and everyone kept an eye out for us kids, whether they knew us or not. The old Armenian lady next door would tell us not to jump in the pile of leaves she had just spent all morning raking because we'd get sick and full of diseases. The English widow on the other side of our house would warn me not to walk along the top of the picket fence because I could fall and hurt myself, which I eventually did, almost losing an eye.

My mother used to wear an apron when she cooked and she often baked cupcakes for the Upsala Street School PTA. The house was always clean and smelled of Pledge furniture polish. She never missed my school functions and checked my papers every day when I came home from school. I had my own room with a full set of encyclopedias and matching furniture. Holidays and birthdays were filled with excitement. All the planning and preparation, building up to the big day. My stepfather worked in the local motor-oil factory during the day and was the head cook nights and weekends at White's Restaurant, a nice family restaurant where we went for special occasions like the night of my dance recital when I was five. Life was stable, safe, and like everyone else's family for that brief few years until the fights began.

My stepfather, Charlie, truly loved my mother. Who else would tolerate all her demands?

"Why can't you get a license and drive like other men? Instead you have to walk everywhere," she would say in a belittling tone. "You're not even handy around the house. You don't even own a damn tool box!"

I remember hearing Charlie pleading with her, "Carole, I work two jobs, day and night to put food on the table, so you and the kids can have a decent place to live. I don't understand what more you want from me." Charlie would try to get her to understand how hard he was trying. "I don't even have a day off anymore."

She would respond with mean things like, "You're so frigging predictable and boring! Why do you have to get up at the same time every day? Why do you have to shave and shine your shoes at the same damn time *every* day?" To add insult to injury, she'd say, "Why can't you have more imagination, dress better, or hold an intelligent conversation? For Christ's sake, you can't even pronounce the word *film* right, no matter how many times I clearly pronounce it for you. It's not 'filim,' it's 'film'!"

The worst arguments were always after he visited his mother, who was enemy number one for my mom. From what I could gather, Charlie had lived with and supported his widowed mother until he was almost thirty years old. His mother did not think much of her son's nineteen-year-old girlfriend, who was divorced with a two-year-old child.

Up until that time, my mother and I had been renting a room in an apartment with a lady and her five children. I stayed with the woman and her kids during the day while my mother worked in the plastics factory that was within walking distance of our apartment building. I remember watching her from the bedroom window as she walked down the street to work.

There was a diner across the street that we would go to and that's where my mother met Charlie. He was a short-order cook and lived within walking distance. The next thing I remember, my mother was married to Charlie, and we moved to the Buffum Street apartment. A few months later, Bob was born. Mom was twenty-one years old, I was four, and life was good.

All that changed when my mother and Charlie split up. At first she would leave me alone with my brother while she went out with her girlfriends. I was six years old and Bob was barely two. One night, I woke up and heard strange voices in the den outside my bedroom. The lights were off and my bedroom door was open. The unfamiliar voices belonged to a man and a woman. They seemed to be breathing heavy and for the most part, the words were muffled. Somehow, I sensed it was not a good time to get out of bed, so I laid low until all the activity subsided and finally fell back to sleep.

For a while, there were different men who stayed over. It was disconcerting to wake up and not know who was in the house. Then one man stayed for a long time and never went to work. His name was Paul. He and Mom spent a lot of time in the bedroom behind closed doors. Unlike Charlie, this man liked to smoke cigarettes, drink beer, lie on the couch during the day with no shirt on and watch sports on television. Pretty soon, we had to leave our cozy life on Esther Street. It was hard to say good-bye but exciting to be moving on to something new. I loved new adventures.

The new apartment was above a corner store on a main street with lots of traffic. The rooms had high ceilings, and narrow windows with faded, yellow window shades. The bathroom had a white porcelain tub with permanent rust stains and dirty claw feet.

Someone had gone to the bathroom in the tub and left it there. The floor had tiny black and white diamond tiles with years of dirt caked between each tile. The toilet was old fashioned, with the water box and pull chain. The toilet seat was black and cracked on one side. What would now be considered retro was old and out of date in the early 1960s.

My new school, Lincoln Street Elementary, was a lot different than the previous one. Mr. Johnson, the principal, stood in the middle of the girls' restroom tapping a yardstick. We all formed a single file line that circled around the cavernous restroom with twenty stalls on either side and sinks on the far end wall. If you had to go to the bathroom, you dropped into a stall and when you finished, you stepped back into the line. If you didn't keep pace or if you were caught talking, you were hit with the yardstick. The kids were tough here, especially the girls. I learned how to get along, even with the meanest kids.

One of my first memories of this school was standing in line in the hallway outside the classroom waiting to walk to the girls' bathroom. The hallway was filled with students as every classroom on that floor had recess at the same time. The principal, as always, walked up and down the hallway with his yardstick in hand. It seemed he was listening for the slightest sound so that he could use that stick on the person who made it.

Not knowing anyone, I felt safe and had no urge to talk or make noise of any kind. That changed when I felt the palm of someone's hand push hard into my shoulder, almost knocking me into the person in front of me. I heard myself begin to utter "Hey...." In that split second, the principal, who was now at the end of the hall, whirled around and began marching in my direction. I pursed my lips and looked straight ahead. He stopped in front of me.

"Are you a new student?" His eyes were piercing and his jaw was tight.

"It's my first day, sir."

He then reminded me, "There is no talking in the hallways at any time, do you understand?" All the while he was thumping the yardstick against his palm.

I nodded that I understood, afraid to even say yes. Once we were outside in the school yard, people went off in different directions to play. Some jumped rope, some played ball, and others ran around playing tag. I didn't know anyone so I went off to the side of the doorway and was about to sit down on the steps when the same rude girl who had pushed me in line made her way toward me. I could feel myself tensing up as I saw the look on her face. This girl, whom I later learned was Brenda Washington, was on a mission and it was obviously not the same as the Welcome Wagon's. Brenda was tall and lanky but she looked tough. As she made her way toward me, people moved out of her way. It was clear that the other kids did not want to mess with her.

I had never been in a fight, and for that matter, I never wanted to find out how well I would do. For some reason, I just knew I would be on the losing end. So this situation called for some quick thinking. I reached into my pocket and just as Brenda reached me, I pulled out my ball and jacks.

She looked down at my hand and asked, "Hey what's that you're holding?"

"Jacks," I answered in my most matter of fact tone of voice, "You want to play?"

She promptly grabbed the ball and jacks out of my hand and sat down next to me. She threw the jacks up in the air, and before you could blink an eye, Brenda and I were playing jacks, and I had made my first friend. From that day forward, no one ever bothered me because they would have to answer to Brenda.

Neither my mother nor her new boyfriend seemed to have a job, and soon we moved yet again to the three-decker apartment building on Castle Street, where my mother was now threatening to throw my brother over the railing.

After several more threats, Paul eventually backed off saying, "Okay, I believe you. Now put the kid back in bed."

I could hear my mother and Paul coming back inside, still arguing but no longer shouting. I heard the door to the third floor porch being closed shut and the dead bolt being turned into place. The danger had passed, and I could feel my heart beating more normally. As I heard my mother close my brother's bedroom door, I remember pulling the covers up over my head, trying to block out the drunken conversation coming from my mother's room. I don't remember if Bob ever woke up that night but it took me a long time to get back to sleep.

The Castle Street apartment was directly across from Castle Hill Park. It was an interesting place for a curious eight-year-old kid. Vacant lots with abandoned cars inhabited the side of the street with the park; the other side of the street was lined with three-story red-brick row houses filled mainly with elderly widows and couples. Our building was the last one on the street, next to a vacant lot. It had two apartments on each floor. Paul's mother and father lived in one apartment. His sister and her family lived in another. His grandmother lived on the first floor by herself with two birds. Her apartment was filled with antique furniture and lace doilies, and it smelled like moth balls all the time.

Every floor had a front porch and a back porch. The back porches on each floor were all connected by stairs running through the middle. The kitchens in each apartment led to the back porch. So inevitably, people would put their empty soda bottles out on the porch, which was a gold mine to an eight-year-old. The large bottles were worth a nickel, and the small ones were worth two cents. Each time my mother sent me to the store, I'd grab as many bottles as I could carry; the large ones were my first preference, of course. I could make as much as twenty-five cents per trip on a good day.

Once we moved to Castle Street, the smells were different. The house was filled with the odor of stale beer and cigarettes. There were always dirty pots and pans on the stove and piles of dishes in the sink. My mother's aprons were replaced with stained housecoats that had snaps down the front and a pocket on either side. It seemed that one pocket was always slightly torn, and she always kept hair pins and dirty tissues in them.

I remember my mother standing in front of me with hair pins sticking out of her mouth. She was fixing my hair for a school play. As she stood in front of me, pulling a bobby pin out of her mouth to put in my hair, I couldn't help but squirm because the smell was so overwhelming. I looked up at her and noticed her hair was oily and stringy. At twenty-four, she looked just like Paul's mother and like many of the older women that lived in our building. They seemed to live in worn housecoats and slippers. Her breath smelled of stale coffee and cigarettes. What happened to my old Mom, the woman who baked, cleaned, and took care of herself and her family?

After a while, I got to know some of the widows who lived on the street. They would be sweeping the stairs or doing yard work when I would pass by on my way to the store. I would offer to purchase items for them since I was going to the store anyway. This would usually earn me a five or ten cent tip plus an apple or some cherry tomatoes. I especially liked running errands for Mrs. Parsons because she was kind to me and always made me feel special. She lived in a basement apartment which was always cooler than outside and smelled of apples and kerosene.

Eventually, I made a friend, Lorraine. She lived around the corner on Main Street in an apartment over the comic book store near Gilrein's Bar. I loved walking by the back door of Gilrein's after five o'clock because the smell of steak permeated the air along with the smooth sounds of live jazz.

Our favorite thing to do was to pretend we were driving the abandoned cars in the vacant lot on my street. There were Cadillacs, Chevys, Fords, and Pontiacs from the 1950s. They were so much fun despite the smell of mildewed upholstery and all the broken glass. I was only limited by my imagination. I would travel all over in my '55 Pontiac convertible and make believe I was far away.

Chapter 4

My mother would always say, "You are the only kid I know who comes back from the store with more money than she left with." How I wish that were true today. But back then, she was right.

I decided I needed to earn more money than I did from cashing in soda bottles and running errands for the neighbors. One day I noticed an ad in a comic book. It boasted how easy I could make money by selling Christmas cards. The card company would send you a kit for fifty cents, and for every pack of cards you sold, you earned a quarter.

I don't remember how much the packs sold for, but I do remember how hard it was to sell the cards during the summer in my neighborhood. I only had two weeks to sell them all and turn in the money. I went out every day for a week and only sold one pack! It was slow going until I went to my maternal grandmother's house for the weekend. She lived in a well-to-do suburb where people planned ahead. My grandmother was a great forward planner too. By Sunday evening, I sold seven of the ten packs and earned a dollar seventy-five. Even though it was good money, I realized I was not cut out to be a Christmas-card salesman, so I decided to return the remaining packs of cards and the money. The instructions from the card company expressly stated not to send cash, which meant I needed my mother's help to get a money order.

When I heard my mother coming down the hall, instead of tucking the money and cards away as I usually did, I left everything on the bed. I had not told her what I was doing because I was sure it would not end well. Although my goal had been to sell all ten packs, I still felt good about selling most of them, and I was hoping she would see merit in the fact that I had earned some money on my own.

When my mother saw the pile of dollar bills on my bed, she looked genuinely surprised. She asked me where I had gotten all the money. I showed her the kit, told her about my hard-won efforts and then explained how I needed her help to return the remaining cards and the money minus my commission. She seemed impressed that I had been able to earn so much money without her even being aware. I felt relieved that she wasn't upset with me.

Then she scooped up the money and before I could digest what she was saying, my earnings had become a loan that she promised to pay back. With each passing day, I grew more and more anxious because the greeting card company was expecting their cards and money. After a few weeks, I began receiving threatening letters in the mail, each one more intimidating that the last.

At first my mother continued to promise to make good but after a few months, she finally told me to forget about the whole thing. She said it was no big deal and the greeting card company was not going to bother going after a little girl for less than twenty-five dollars. Night after night, I would wake up in a cold sweat having dreamed I had been hauled off to jail in handcuffs. Long after the greeting card incident, I continued to have dreams of being imprisoned. I'd wake up in a cold sweat.

I was in the third grade now, so my mother began to let me go to church on Sundays by myself. She would give me coins to drop in the collection basket and send me on my way. I would walk down Castle Street to Main Street past the Waldorf Cafeteria, where the most inviting smells of breakfast would remain in my head the whole time I was in church.

I don't know what made me decide to only drop two dimes in the basket and hold back the rest, but I did. After church, I headed straight for the Waldorf Cafeteria, climbed up on a stool, rested my elbows on the counter and reached for a menu. I scanned the menu for the items that I could afford and decided on an English muffin with jelly for twenty cents and a glass of fresh squeezed orange juice for a dime. It was by far the best tasting English muffin because they toasted it on the grill, which made it golden brown. The soft, rich creamery butter melted evenly across the muffin and the two packets of grape jelly were exactly the right amount to entirely cover the two halves. I savored every bite and saved the orange juice for the end.

One Sunday, as I started to get ready for church, my mother came in to my room, "Carole, I want you to take your brother with you today."

Bob was almost four years old now, but I wasn't sure he could walk the whole way to Saint Paul's Cathedral.

"Mom, he's too slow and I can't carry him if he gets tired. He'll make me late."

Listening to none of it, she insisted. "You will take him with you or you won't go at all!"

I looked at Bob all dressed up in his big boy pants and sweater. My mother had used water to comb his hair to tame his unruly blond curls.

"Okay, we'd better get going or we're going to be late."

Taking my hand, Bob looked up at me and said, "Okay, Ca."

It seemed that it took Bob forever to walk down the three flights of stairs, but once we were on the street, he did much better. The cathedral was located downtown, almost a mile away. I could usually make it in twenty minutes, but Bob's little legs got us there after the service had already started. This was a new experience for my little brother, and he sat very quietly taking everything in.

When I would kneel, he would kneel. All in all, given his age, Bob was taking direction well. So well, in fact, when the basket came around, I told him,

"Hang on to the quarter, Bob."

He looked up at me. "But Mom said it was for church. Doesn't God need it?" he asked innocently.

"Yes, that's why I'm giving Him one of mine but you need to hang on to yours for what comes later."

Surprisingly enough, Bob listened and put the quarter back into his pocket. As we walked down the hill to Main Street, I contemplated whether I should risk sharing my favorite place with Bob. But he was my brother, after all, and he deserved a good breakfast every now and again too.

When we went inside the Waldorf Cafeteria, I helped Bob onto a stool then climbed onto the one next to him.

"What's this place, Ca?"

"This is where people go after church."

I pointed out a few people that I had seen during Mass. "See, that lady with the black veil on her hat? She was at church with us. That man was, too. Hey, are you hungry, Bob?"

Nodding affirmatively, he said, "Yeah! I want waffles."

Reaching my hand out to him I said, "We don't have enough for waffles, but if you give me your quarter, we can both get English muffins and jelly. Do you want milk or juice?"

Eyes wide with anticipation, he said, "Juice!"

It was nice to have my brother with me. I always felt lonely having breakfast by myself. Now I had someone to share it with. We ate every last crumb, wiped our mouths, and I helped Bob off the stool. I buttoned his sweater, and we headed out the door for the long walk home.

"Did you like going to breakfast, Bob?"

Without hesitation, he said, "Yeah."

Here was the hard part. "Okay, well let's just keep it to ourselves."

He looked up at me he asked, "Why?"

Looking straight ahead, I answered, "Well, Mom might not understand."

"You mean because we spent God's money?"

"I mean because she didn't give us the money for church and breakfast. So let's just not mention it, okay?"

Bob glanced away as he said, "Okay."

By the time we made it home, it was close to noon, and my mother was in the kitchen washing clothes and boiling water on the stove. Bob ran into the kitchen and I could hear my mother ask him,

"So how was church?"

Excitedly, Bob told her, "It was big and echoed a lot. They played music and burned candles. Then we ate English muffins and jelly at the place but I'm not supposed to tell you."

Lying in bed that night after being punished for the rest of the day, I remember feeling so guilty for cheating God out of sixty cents, and I vowed to make it up some day. I intended to keep my promise.

Chapter 5

By the time I was ten, my mother and Paul had two children together. In addition to my brother and me, one of Paul's children from a previous marriage, Paul Jr., was living with us. Paul Jr. was six, the same age as Bobby. Together, the two boys were a handful, along with Kay, who was two, and Kennedy, who was just a year old.

We had moved three more times since we had lived on Castle Street. I was in my fourth elementary school and by all accounts, I should have transferred to a fifth school closer to the run-down apartment we lived in on Waverly Street. But I chose to walk the mile or so to Lamartine Street School because I really loved my fifth grade teacher, Mr. Friedman.

One of my jobs around the house was to do the laundry, which I truly hated because it took so long. First, I had to pull the wringer-washer out and hook up the drainage hose to the sink. Then I had to fill the tub with water. The one saving grace was that it could agitate by itself. Putting the clothes through the wringer was the best part. I loved seeing the water squeezed out of each piece. The clothes were all scrunched up when they came out the other side.

Then I filled the clothesline row by row. I started with the diapers and the baby clothes and hung them on the inside line because it was the shortest. Then I turned the clothesline slightly to fill up the next section until I got to the outside rows, where I hung the sheets and towels.

Washing clothes, sheets, and towels for me and the kids seemed to take forever. The diapers were the worst, especially the older ones that I had forgotten to rinse out. They often contained moving surprises.

Another challenge in those days was figuring out what to feed the kids, for which I was also responsible. The shelves in our pantry were nearly always empty. We only received USDA commodities once a month. I really couldn't remember the last time my mother actually went to a grocery store. She never did weekly shopping because that was too expensive. Usually, whenever my mother could scrape together a few dollars, she'd send me to the Honey Farms on the corner. When things were really bad, she'd call her mother who would send my grandfather over to drop off bread and milk money for the babies. Grandma Helen was always good that way, making sure we had clothes and food whenever my mother asked her for help, which I suspected was quite often

Paul and my mother would often go to the local bar at night but forget to pick up food for us while they were out. Sometimes Paul would give me a few dollars to send me to the store for a quart of beer, a pack of cigarettes, and a bag of candy bars. I never understood why there just wasn't enough to buy everything we needed. When Paul found work occasionally and they could buy food, they couldn't afford to buy the same thing for all of us. My mother would make two separate meals, one for us and one for her and Paul. While all the kids were eating hot dogs and beans in the kitchen, my mother and Paul would eat steak and fries in the living room while they watched TV.

There was never enough food or money to go around. That's why I had to give back a dress Grandma Helen bought me at Filene's for my birthday. On one occasion, Grandma Helen gave my mother money to buy the Camp Fire Girls' uniform that I wanted desperately. But now that there were so many little ones, my mother needed the money to get us through until pay day. She always promised to make it up to me. She would pay me back one of these days.

It was pretty silly, when you think of it, to want to spend money on a Camp Fire Girl's uniform when there was hardly anything in the fridge or the pantry. There wasn't anyone to do the activities with me, and the uniform was just the beginning. I'd never be able to go to summer camp or get the badges. We didn't have any of the things that were on the arts and crafts list. My mom was right. What was I thinking?

I remember looking forward to every other Sunday. They were the absolute best days of the week. That's when my dad or his mother, Grandma Marie, would come and pick me up to spend the day with them. Since I was the only child from that marriage, the other kids did not go with me. Grandma Marie drove a royal blue 1956 Chevy Beach Wagon, and she always brought my Uncle Henry with her. Henry was a year older than me, and he always showed off and made me laugh. I'd start getting ready hours before they were due to arrive.

With four little ones, my mother always had a long list of chores for me to do before I left:

"Don't forget to change your sister's diaper." "Did you give Kennedy her bottle? "Don't forget to bring the laundry in off the back porch. It's going to rain." "Remember to take out the trash."

All the while, I'd be watching out the front porch to see if the Chevy was in sight. The minute I saw it, my heart would sing. I loved going to my paternal grandparents' home because there were always so many fun things to do.

Grandma Marie and Henry would usually pick me up right after church, and we would go back to the house for Sunday dinner. My grandparents' one-story, two-bedroom bungalow was built on a large peninsula of land surrounded by Coe's Pond. It used to be a summer cottage that my grandparents winterized and turned into a year round home. Tall pines landscaped their backyard with a man-made shiner pond off to the right behind the house. They sold shiners and night crawlers for bait to customers who rented boats to fish on Coe's Pond. Grandpa had hung a tire swing from one of the trees that overlooked the shiner pond. I spent hours swinging as high as I could go, out over the water.

Directly behind the house was a canvas covered glider with two benches that faced each other. I can recall countless sunny afternoons when Grandma, Henry, and me would sit in the swing, gently rocking back and forth while talking quietly and listening to the sounds of nature that surrounded us. Grandpa would stop and talk for a bit too but he was always busy with some project around the house or the yard. His list was never-ending, but he seemed to like it that way.

The smell of Grandma's cooking would make me so hungry that you could hear my stomach growling all the way from the living room. Grandma's specialty was Italian food, but everything she made was mouth-watering. When the meal was finally ready, we would gather around the lime-green Formica-topped kitchen table with chrome legs and matching vinyl-upholstered chairs, which remained in their pine paneled kitchen well into the 1970s.

After dinner we'd swim or row around the pond. In the winter we would skate on the shiner pond, which made an excellent rink when it froze.

The neighborhood kids would drop by and join us because there was always fun to be had. Sometimes, we'd go to the local miniature golf course, and Henry would let me win every now and then. Once in a great while, on the way back we'd stop at the local Dairy Queen for a sundae. Life was always better at Grandma and Grandpa's house.

School that year was the best year ever. Mr. John Friedman, my fifth-grade teacher, was the youngest, most enthusiastic teacher I had ever met. I really loved his class because he made learning exciting. He cared about each one of us and showed it by walking up and down the rows, taking care to look over our work. He always made helpful and encouraging comments and took a personal interest in each one of us.

Compared to the more traditional teachers I encountered up to that point in my young life, Mr. Friedman had many innovative ideas. He believed in teaching more than just reading and writing so that we would be successful in life. For example, he had a hygiene chart that listed all the students' names and next to each name there were boxes to check off the various daily personal grooming activities such as bathing, teeth brushing, using deodorant, and so forth. I remember really working hard to make sure I did all the things on the list. Sometimes, even though I took a bath before I went to bed, I would still not smell fresh when I went to school in the morning. This was because my little sister, Kay, shared the twin bed with me and she had kidney problems. I would often wake up in the middle of the night and find myself lying on a wet bed. I would change my sister and the sheets, take off my wet clothes and lay them out to dry and wash up but somehow the smell remained.

Another problem was socks—I never seemed to have enough for the week, so I would have to recycle a pair or two until I could do laundry on the weekend. My boots were rubber and I did not have any shoes. This meant that I had to wear rubber boots inside the warm classroom all day. Thinking back, it became clear why Mr. Friedman would

double check my answers on the hygiene board.
One day he even addressed the class about telling
the truth. I remember wondering why.

I recall Mr. Friedman introducing two visitors
to our class, a young couple named Emily and John.
They were in graduate school and needed a few
students to help them with their thesis. Mr.
Friedman picked me and three other students to
participate. Over the next several weeks, we would
get to leave the classroom and go to the training
room where Emily and John had set up several
different activities for us to choose from and
perform. Afterward, they would ask us questions.
There were no right or wrong answers, and I really
do not remember the point of the activities or the
outcome.

What I do remember is that two of us were
chosen to go on a few field trips. On one trip the
couple took us to the brand new library downtown.
We walked there after school and walked through
the plaza at the chamber of commerce, which had a
beautiful fountain. We stopped to throw a penny
and make a wish. Music was coming from the
speakers and the sun beaming on the spraying water
created a beautiful rainbow. It felt magical, but the
best part was yet to come. As we made our way
across the plaza, past the blossoming cherry trees,
then down the cobblestone sidewalk, the new
library came into view.

It was a beautiful building with clean, crisp,
modern lines and wall-to-wall glass on every level.
I couldn't wait to run up the wide, polished, white
granite steps. The impressive building was a

departure from the industrial-era architecture that dominated the City of Worcester. It smelled so new when we went inside. Instead of cold granite floors, the lobby had beautiful plush carpet.

Then the most amazing thing happened. John and Emily helped us each get a library card that would allow us to borrow up to six books for two weeks at a time. The best part was that it was free and the library was open seven days a week. Emily said,

"Now that you know how to get here, you can come anytime you want as long as you have your card and remain a member in good standing. You have to return books by the due date or pay a nickel for each day a book is late."

I vowed I would always be a member in good standing. Then Emily and John taught us how to use the Dewey decimal system to find the books we needed for research projects, and they gave us a tour of this wonderful building. When they let us have free time to pick out what we wanted to read, I immediately went to historical fiction, drama and romance sections and took out the thickest book I could find: *Gone With the Wind,* because I didn't want it to end. I began reading right there on the floor in between the books stacked high up all around me. This was by far the best gift anyone had ever given me. Reading unlocked my imagination and took me to far away places. It was my daily escape.

At the end of the semester, Emily and John invited the two of us to their tiny apartment to make a spaghetti dinner. We had different tasks and worked together in their little kitchen.

I was stirring the spaghetti when Emily asked me, "Carole, have you thought about going to college?"

"Oh, my family would never be able to afford to send me."

Then Emily shared the best piece of information that anyone had given me up to that point in my young life. She told me how neither of their families had enough money to send them to college so they both applied for and received scholarships based on financial need. That's how they had gotten their undergraduate degrees. Later on, they both had been awarded teaching fellowships to pay for grad school. From that day forward, I had a sense of hope and excitement for the future because I knew I would go to college, too.

College seemed far away though because that year was a tough one. Paul occasionally found work with a friend who owned a dump truck. They did salvage work, which was dependent upon the weather. There was lots of down time with the ever-changing New England climate. When he did work, there was enough food for three meals a day, but there was also more money for beer. I disliked Friday nights because instead of coming home after work, Paul headed straight for the tavern after getting paid. If he was not home by eight o'clock, my mother would send me down to the bar to get money for rent and groceries.

Since kids were not allowed inside, I would have to hang around the door for someone to come out so that person could go back in and get Paul. When Paul finally appeared in the doorway, he was usually well on his way to tying one on. I would tell him what my mother wanted and sometimes he would peel off several bills from a folded wad that he somehow managed to get out of his pocket without stumbling. He would give me the money, pat me on the head, and tell me to let my mother know he would be home in a bit. Other times, he would tell me in no uncertain terms to tell my mother where she could go and what she could do. None of which I could ever repeat to my mother if I wanted to keep my teeth intact.

Whenever I came home without the money, she would go out looking for him. This was never good because eventually they would arrive home drunk and continue the argument. If the kids were not already in bed, I would herd them off to one room and get them settled down behind closed doors. Once they were safe, I would put my ear to the door to see if the coast was clear. Most of the time, you could hear every slurred word, loud and clear. Somehow the four letter words were always the clearest.

Some Friday night fights would escalate to pushing, shoving, punching, and slapping each other. I usually ended up in the middle, yelling at Paul to leave my mother alone and eventually they would stop. One night stands out more than the rest. That was the night I came into the kitchen after getting the kids quickly into the bedroom to see my mother standing in the middle of the kitchen, waving a butcher knife in the air screaming, "I'm going to kill you!" Her arm was bleeding.

Paul was shouting obscenities and telling her, "Give it your best shot."

She lunged at him yelling, "You bastard!"

He dodged her and ran out the back door, heading towards the stairs. She was right behind him and managed to grab onto his t-shirt, tearing it right off his back. She pushed him, and I could hear him stumble and fall down the stairs. I picked up the phone and dialed the operator to get the police. As I was telling the operator what the emergency was, my mother came from behind, grabbed the phone out of my hand and slammed it down. She slapped me across the face, screaming,

"Are you stupid?"

Then I became the target of her rage. Long after the physical pain subsided, I never forgot all the things I felt toward my mother that night. It was a tipping point. I slipped out of the house and found the nearest pay phone. I dialed the number of the one person I knew really cared about us, my maternal grandmother, Grandma Helen. As I looked up and down the street to make sure my mother was nowhere in sight, the familiar nurturing voice of my grandmother came on the line.

"Hello."

"Grandma, it's me. Grandma, can I come live with you? Things are really bad here, and I can't live here anymore. Please, Grandma."

"Carole Jane, things can't be that bad."

She didn't seem to understand. How could she not know how bad things were at our house? I guess my mother had done a good job of hiding the truth.

"Grandma, Mom and Paul have terrible fights. I tried to call the police, and Mommy slapped me across the face. They drink a lot and we never have enough food in the house. They make me stay home from school to take care of the kids and my grades are falling, Grandma. I can't live like this anymore."

"Carole Jane, things seem just worse than they are because you're upset. Everything will look better in the morning."

The next day, they were both in the living room watching TV, eating snacks and drinking beer. They were the best of friends again. It seemed like the night before had never happened. Paul came out to the kitchen to find me reading a book in my favorite chair in the corner. He started asking me,

"Why are you so lazy? Instead of sitting on your ass, why don't you do the laundry, wash the dishes, and sweep the floor?"

I remember thinking how grateful I was that he couldn't read my thoughts as I got up and started doing what he told me to do. While I was out on the porch hanging clothes, the scenes from the night before kept flashing through my head. I kept replaying my mother's words from the night before,

"Are you stupid?"

I finished hanging out the last piece of laundry, crept quietly down the back stairs, and hopped on the rusty old bike the tenant on the second floor had given me. I started peddling as fast as I could and did not stop until the chain broke about a mile away. When the bike rolled to a stop, I jumped off and started running until I reached a pay phone. I called my dad's house, but no one answered so I just kept on running. I don't remember how long it took but I remember arriving on my dad's back porch and knocking on the door. The look of shock and surprise on my stepmother's face when she saw me was telltale, but there was no turning back now.

After several stressful days of hiding every time my mother came knocking on the door, we finally got a hearing before a judge. I remember the judge calling me into his chambers to ask,

"Carole, how do you feel about your mother?"

To this day, I remember answering: "I love my mother; I just can't live with her."

The judge granted temporary custody to Grandma Marie since my dad could not afford the legal fees.

Chapter 6

Some of the fondest memories from my childhood revolve around the time I spent with Baby, my dad's black Belgian shepherd. Baby and I became fast friends during the year I lived with my dad and his family. She was a port in a storm on many occasions as it was often difficult to fit in to a ready-made family that was not expecting me to land on their door step. Although I tried my best to please my dad and his wife, I was eleven years old and not used to the strict expectations that my stepmother, Mary, had for household chores.

"Now that you are living with us, you will be expected to help out. You will earn a weekly allowance of fifty cents each Saturday," Mary said as she handed me a calendar. "You will follow this calendar for taking baths and washing your hair. You need to make your bed every day, clear the table, do the dishes, make sure the sink and stove are clean, and burn the trash in the barrel behind the house each night."

I was no stranger to chores and eager to help. So I said, "Okay, no problem."

The next day when I came home from school, Mary was waiting for me in the kitchen, "Come here. I'm going to show you how to make a bed."

She pointed to the middle of the bed that sagged because the mattress was old. "You need to pull the sheets and blanket until they're taut and tuck them in like this." She grabbed the edges of the bedding, pulling it tightly and forcefully tucking them in between the mattress and the box spring. "That's how I want you to do it, okay?"

Wanting to make her happy, I answered, "Yes, I can do that."

Then she said, "Now, come here," as she walked over to the kitchen sink, I followed closely behind. She pointed to the strainer in the drain.

"You see that?"

Being a kid, I said, "You mean the strainer?"

I could hear the annoyance in her voice as she pulled the strainer out of the drain, grabbed my hand, turned the palm up, and emptied the food particles into my hand. "Doing the dishes right means emptying the strainer into the garbage bin, got it?"

How did I miss that, I wondered?

"One more thing, go over to the broiler and open it." I walked over and slid it open.

Looking at the dirty broiler pan from last night's meal, I said, "Oh geez! I'm sorry, I forgot." I took it over to the sink and began to scrub the grease and dried up charcoal remains of the hamburgers we had the night before. I could see how disappointed Mary was in me.

"I'll do better, Mary. I really am sorry."

As she stood at the kitchen table, folding towels, she explained, "Each time you forget or don't do it right, money will be deducted from the fifty cents allowance we agreed on each week. It will cost you a quarter if you forget the broiler, a nickel each time you forget to empty the strainer, and a dime if the bed is not made correctly, understand?"

Trying hard not to cry, "Yes, I understand."

As the weeks, passed, I thought I must be doing fairly well, until the day I came home from school and saw a paper towel with something on it lying on top of my pillow. As I got closer, I could see particles of food from the strainer in the sink that I had obviously forgotten, once again.

I went to the kitchen to throw the garbage away. Mary was sitting at the kitchen table, smoking a cigarette and working on one of her craft projects that arrived each month. The kids were in the den playing and my brother Mario went outside to play. I thought about doing the same and just as I turned to go, Mary said without turning to look at me,

"You forgot the broiler again so that's $.30 that will be deducted from your allowance this week."

Despite my trials and tribulations with household chores, I loved getting to know my dad's children, who were all under the age of five at the time. Almost immediately, the youngest two were eager to have me carry them around. The baby, Stephen, would climb out of his crib to come and sleep with me at night, much to Mary's dismay. When the two year-old, Rochelle, fell one day and started to cry, she turned toward me and raised her arms for me to pick her up so I ran to her.

A stern voice from behind me warned,

"She's my kid and I will take care of her."
I stepped aside to let Mary pick up the baby.

A few weeks later, I came home to find my bedding in a heap on top of the bed. I was sure I had made the bed in the morning before I left. Mary was in the den, sitting in the rocking chair by the window. She was crocheting while she watched TV. The smoke from her cigarette rose from the ashtray on the window sill, filling the room with haze as the sun streamed through the three front windows. I could tell she was annoyed with me because she did not look up when I came to the door way. I stood there awkwardly waiting for her to look up.

After the longest time she asked, "Did you want something?"

Nervously, I answered, "Mary, I am really sorry I didn't make the bed right."

Staring straight ahead at the TV, she took a drag off her cigarette and said, "I don't need you to be sorry. I need you to do things right. I am sick and tired of having to show you the same things over and over. I know you're not stupid."

I don't know why I couldn't do anything right. I really was a disappointment. I truly wanted Mary to love me and to treat me the same as if I was her own child. I desperately wanted to belong. I even tried to call her *Mom*, but it was hard to remember.

As an escape, I went for long hikes in the woods behind my dad's house. Baby was my hiking companion. Before heading off on our usual walk, I would often grab two ice cream sandwiches out of the freezer on the back porch. One for Baby, and one for me. When Baby would see me heading for the path in the woods, she would come running. Sometimes she would lead and other times she would patiently follow, but we never stopped until we reached our special spot in the woods. There was a slight clearing and a babbling brook running downstream through the woods. I would sit on my favorite rock and Baby would sit in front of me. We would both enjoy our ice cream. Baby licked the wrapper clean every time.

We would sit for hours, listening to the water trickle over the rocks. I loved the solitude of the woods and being surrounded by nature. Baby never bothered the squirrels that danced through the branches, nor did she run after the deer. She seemed content to listen to me talk as I poured out my heart to her. She was my best friend, so gentle and loving but protective whenever a stranger approached.

When I started school at the end of the summer, I was worried that Baby would be lonely during the day. My younger half-brother, Mario, was starting kindergarten that year. Baby would walk us down to the bottom of the hill, and I would tell her to stay. She would sit and watch us until I couldn't see her anymore. Mary told me Baby would return on her own each day, then at three o'clock, she would be waiting for us as we came up the hill. She was the best dog ever. She was always happy to see me.

My dad lived in a three-story house and during the time that I lived with him and his family, Mary's parents, the Stevens, and her sister lived on the second floor. I loved visiting Mr. and Mrs. Stevens because they had an upright piano in their parlor. Although I had never taken any formal lessons, I enjoyed creating my own songs. My dad heard me play once and I guess he thought I had a little talent because he called Mary and told her to come upstairs to hear me play. A few months back, I had asked if I could take piano lessons, but Mary told me money was tight and that they could not afford it.

About a week after my dad and Mary listened to me play, they told me I would be taking lessons with the Sisters of Mercy at the convent downtown across from St. Paul's Cathedral, where I used to go to church when I lived with my mother. I was so excited that I readily agreed to practice an hour every day. I counted down the days until Saturday and my first lesson.

When Saturday morning finally rolled around, I was up bright and early. I took the bus downtown and walked one block to the convent. I was forty-five minutes early, but it gave me a chance to listen to the other students playing in the individual glass studios that lined both sides of the hallway. I could hear the tick tock of what I later learned was a metronome to keep the beat. You could set it to any tempo you wanted: four-four, two-four, and so forth.

After a while, more students arrived and joined me on the bench in the waiting room. Then right at ten o'clock, the doors opened and all the students left; the ones who were waiting went into their studios. Just when I was about to get up and go ask someone where I needed to go, an older nun dressed in a long traditional habit walked towards the waiting room.

"You must be Carole?" I nodded, a little nervous. "I'm Sr. Mary Barbara, Carole. Follow me to this last studio on the right with the big grand piano. Take a seat on the bench, please."

I went over to the bench and carefully slid behind the ivory keys, careful not to hit any, as I took my jacket off.

Sr. Mary Barbara took out an index card with my name and the date on it. "Have you ever taken piano lessons before, Carole?" She checked off the boxes on the card then began to explain how to read the music on the sheet in front of me. Once she had explained how the notes, lines, and spaces correlated with the keys on the piano, she played the first tune I was to learn. She explained how I should set the metronome to keep pace with the time in which the piece was written. It was awkward at first but after a while, my fingers began to move effortlessly along the keyboard in time. In time, I knew without looking where to find the notes. I practiced every day on the piano in my dad's basement. Soon I built up quite a repertoire of pieces as I progressed through the various levels.

It became so easy that even when I played every song I had learned in addition to practicing my new piece, I struggled to practice for the full hour. By the end of the week, I was so bored sitting in front of the piano trying to make the hour stretch that I began to look for excuses to get through it. I'd go upstairs to go to the bathroom, then return and play a few more pieces. All of sudden my throat would become dry, so I'd go upstairs to get a drink of water. I'd go back downstairs and play several more pieces, until the water made me have to go to the bathroom once again. None of this escaped Mary's watchful eye,

"Carole, you will need to practice another fifteen minutes to account for all the time you've wasted. Stop wasting time and practice!"

I went back downstairs and played every song I had learned over the last six months. I looked at the clock and saw I still had ten minutes left so I began to look through my books and read about the various composers: Mozart, Chopin, Beethoven, Bach, Wagner, Haydn, all the classical greats. By the time I finished reading the brief bios on each one, the ten minutes had more than passed so I shut the lights off and went upstairs.

It was just before 9:30 in the morning when I walked into the kitchen to tell Mary I was going for a bike ride.

"You're grounded for the rest of the day. I told you to stop wasting time and to practice. You ignored me. Go sit in the chair in the corner of the bedroom and don't come out until I tell you to."

"But I wasn't wasting time, I was reading my music theory books," I said pleadingly.

Mary was having none of it. All day long the kids ran in and out of the room, wondering why I couldn't get out the chair. As the day went on, they poked fun and taunted me as children do. It was so humiliating and as the afternoon turned into evening, Mary still would not give me permission to get out of the chair. The plan was to have me sit there until my dad came home. It was pay day, which meant he could be quite late since he often stopped for a beer or two with friends.

It was well after eight o'clock that night when I heard the truck pull into the driveway. I had been sitting in the chair for more than thirteen hours. I could hear my dad's footsteps on the stairs leading to the back door, and I felt myself tensing up. When he came through the back door, Mary was waiting for him.

"What happened? You said you'd be home by six. I had dinner waiting for you."

As my father hung up his coat on the rack in the hallway, he said, "I ran into Leon and Dickie," as he walked past the room I shared with my two stepsisters. I could tell by his speech that he'd had plenty to drink.

"Come over here, Mary and give me a big fat kiss," he said playfully. But Mary was not in a playful mood.

"Carole's grounded and has been sitting in the chair since this morning."

"Now what did she do?" I could hear the anger in his voice,

"She's wasting time instead of practicing. I don't understand why we're spending the money for lessons on a kid who doesn't appreciate it." As she walked towards the bedroom, the anger was obvious.

"Dinner's on the stove, heat it up yourself."
I heard his fist bang down on the table.
"Damn it!"
Then I heard him heading toward me.
"Carole, get out here!"

Afraid of what was coming next, I went out to the kitchen and stood before my father,

"Yes, Dad?"

"Mary tells me you're not practicing the piano like you're supposed to, is that right?"

"Yes, Dad."

"How many times do we have to keep telling you the same thing?" Before I could answer, I felt the pain, then heard my glasses land on the other side of the room. The rest was a blur. My dad had never hit me before. I'm not sure which hurt more.

Through my tears I heard him yell,

"Are you going to practice an hour every day?"

"Yes, Dad," trying not to let him see me cry.

"Get to bed!" His face was so red, it was scary. I wasted no time getting out of the line of fire.

Mary came out of the bedroom and I could hear my dad, "Are you happy now? I took care of her."

"That's not what I wanted you to do." She sounded annoyed with my dad.

"What am I supposed to do? Every time I turn around, you're telling me what she's doing wrong. What else do you want me to do?" I could hear the anger and frustration in his voice.

"Oh, so now it's my fault?" Mary said.

The next thing I heard was the door to their bedroom being slammed shut. The next several days were like walking on egg shells around Mary, but I made sure I practiced the full hour every day, made my bed, did the dishes right, and did not get in her way.

Adjusting to a new family environment is difficult under the best of circumstances, but my situation was complicated by the guilt that plagued me from leaving my younger brothers and sisters behind. I experienced nightmares and sleep walking episodes in the weeks and months after I left my mother and the kids. I would cry myself to sleep because I worried about who would protect them now that I was not there. Who would change their diapers and make sure they were fed? Who would shield them from the screaming and yelling? Who would keep them from seeing the horrible fights? What would happen to them without me there?

I have been plagued with a sense of guilt my entire life. I loved them so much! They were my babies, and I left defenseless babies in that horrible environment with adults who had no business having children. I let them down. How could I do that?

For the better part of a year, I would get phone calls from my brother and sisters. My mother would dial my dad's number and put them on the phone. They would ask, "When are you coming home, Ca? We miss you. Don't you love us anymore? Can we come and stay with you?"

During one of these calls, my mother told me she wanted to leave Paul and go back to school for nursing. She said she could not do it without my help. My unplanned arrival on my dad's doorstep had rocked my stepmother's world. They had four kids at that point and did not have room for a fifth. It seemed I could never do the right thing where my stepmother was concerned. She seemed angry all the time. She and my father were arguing a lot, and my dad was drinking more.

After an unusually turbulent weekend, I tried to apologize to Mary for causing so much tension in the house. Before I could finish, she shot back, "We never fought before you came!"

I stayed awake all night thinking about the babies I had left behind and the problems I was causing for my father and his family. I left the next morning before sunrise. I walked down the hill to Mill Street and caught the first of two buses that took me back to my brothers and sisters who needed me.

Chapter 7

My mother's promise was short-lived and Paul was not out of her life for good. In less than a year, I was sitting in Father Tobias's office at St. Paul's rectory. I attended seventh grade at St. Paul's and Fr. Tobias oversaw the school. I was telling him about how dysfunctional my home life had become while living with my mother and letting him know that I had a foster home lined up but Father Tobias insisted,

"I will have to call your paternal grandparents because they still have legal custody of you."

"They are going to be angry with me for going back to my mother," I explained.

Dialing the number to my grandparents' home, Father Tobias responded, "Well that can't be helped. They will need to relinquish custody before I can place you in a foster home, Carole."

As I predicted, they were not happy to be called by the priest and made it very clear to him how they felt. He asked,

"Are you willing to relinquish custody so that Carole can go into a foster home?"

My grandmother Marie answered, "We can't do that. What will people say? She will come to live with us until she's eighteen, whether she likes it or not. When she turns eighteen, she can get the hell out. We don't care what she does after that."

Chapter 8

Living with my dad's parents was easier in some respects. There were no small children to care for, they did not drink and they were home every night. Since they were already raising their son Henry, who was just a year older than I was, they were already familiar with the educational and social activities of a teenager. Henry was the apple of their eye, and being the youngest and only child at home, they lavished all their attention and resources on him.

They were also overly germ-conscious, so everything had to be spotless. No shoes could be worn in the house, and Lysol was my grandmother's best friend.

The summer before high school, I immersed myself in the reading list, got lots of swimming in, and slimmed down to a size ten. Church was also a regular part of my life. I went every Sunday with Henry and my grandparents. I continued to attend St. Paul's elementary school. Life felt more stable. I loved playing cards and board games with my grandfather whenever we got the chance. Just when I thought that I finally belonged, I would be reminded that I was a temporary guest.

As I entered school that fall and the weather began to grow cold, I needed a new winter coat. My grandmother was reading the paper one day after dinner and looked at me over her reading glasses.

"Eddy's is having a sale on midi coats and winter boots. Want to take a ride down there?"

I could not believe my ears! I had wanted a midi coat forever. "Can we?" I asked incredulously.

My grandmother put down the paper and stood up to go get her coat,

"They close at nine so we've got plenty of time. Let's go!"

I was so excited, I could hardly contain myself. All my friends had midi coats and new boots, and I felt so outdated with the old hand-me-down stadium jacket that Mary had worn in high school. I would rather go to school with just a sweater than wear that old thing, even with the cold New England winter we were experiencing. When we got to Eddy's on Park Avenue, I ran to the juniors section, and it took me all of five minutes to find the coat I wanted. It was a midi length, A-line, button-down-the-front, cranberry wool coat with a hood and side slit pockets. The back pleat allowed for easy sitting without pulling on the buttons. It fit me perfectly and I loved it.

My grandmother turned toward the shoe department and said, "We might as well look at some boots since we're here."

I was surprised that she was being so generous. The coat was more than enough so I said,

"Gram, are you sure?" as I followed her to the boot section.

She turned and said, "Why not? They're on sale, too."

Who was I to argue? After trying on several pair, I finally settled on some dark brown leather, knee-length boots. They looked very nice with the coat, and I was ecstatic. In the car on the way home, I was so tickled and delighted,

"Grandma, thanks so much for taking me to Eddy's! I love my new coat and boots. I can't wait to wear them to school tomorrow!"

Looking straight ahead over the steering wheel, she said, "I'm glad you like them." When we got home, she took off her coat and shoes then went to the cupboard and pulled out a pocket size notebook. She opened her purse and took out the receipts. She began to write the date and the amounts in the notebook then she turned to me and said,

"We'll use this to keep track of the payments."

Payments? What did she mean? They didn't do this with my Uncle Henry. She went on,

"So last week you earned $12 from babysitting for the Johnsons. How much of a down payment do you want to make?"

As I previously mentioned, my grandparents lived on a pond, and, as a side business, they rented boats and sold bait. They earned enough money every year to go to Florida in the winter during school break. I had never been to Florida, but it sure sounded pretty with orange groves, lots of sunshine, and beautiful beaches. As the time drew near, my grandparents began to prepare for the big trip. It was so exciting to hear them plan where they would go first, whom they would visit, what they would see, and what they would take on the trip.

About a week before they were to leave, we were sitting at the dinner table discussing the trip. The dog was under the table and all of sudden; I wondered aloud, "Who's going to take care of Prince?"

Without skipping a beat, my grandfather said, "You will. You'll be staying with your father while we're gone, you can come by several times a day to let Prince out and to feed him."

"With the new baby, there are five kids now and there is nowhere for me to sleep. Can I at least sleep here at night?"

He looked at me sternly and clearly let me know, "You are not allowed to stay here while we are gone."

Christmas came and went, and while I was initially disappointed that I was not included on the trip to Florida, I was able to make a lot of extra babysitting money with all the holiday parties. Moreover, it was fun watching the little ones open their presents on Christmas Day. Henry and my grandparents were back the week after Christmas and soon life was back to normal.

Henry was on the church basketball team and sang in the boys' choir, so I decided to join the girls' choir. There were thirty girls trying out and only ten openings. My chances were slim, but I thought I would give it a shot anyway. I practiced the hymns in Latin every day after school.

The night before tryouts, we were at the dinner table and Henry asked, "So why are you spending so much time learning the hymns?"

Surprised that he was interested, I answered, "Choir try outs are tomorrow after school and there's a lot of competition this year."

My grandfather took a drink of his water, swallowed and looked at me, "How do you plan on getting back and forth to the practices if you do get chosen?"

Frankly, I had not thought about it since my grandparents drove Henry everywhere he wanted to go.

"I can walk. No problem."

Thinking ahead he said, "When it's below freezing or dark out?"

Realizing he wanted to make a point, I said, "Not a problem."

Closing the loop, he offered, "If you want a ride, it will cost you $1 each way, just let me know in advance."

I enjoyed choir so much, it was worth paying the occasional $1 to get there when the weather was bad. In fact, in addition to choir, I joined the cheerleading squad, went to catechism classes every week and church on Sundays. During Lent, I went to Mass every morning on the way to school. I felt a connection with my friends, the religious community at school, and the church. There was a certain comfort in the familiar rituals, formal prayer, songs in Latin, and the continual challenge to obey the Ten Commandments. I felt I was on the right path, the path that would lead to a better life.

Chapter 9

After that chance meeting with the young married grad-school couple when I was ten years old, the notion of going to college was a given. My goal was to study occupational therapy and follow in the footsteps of my elementary school mentor, Ms. Eastern. It was obvious that my grandparents also valued a good education.

I had seen the college application process first hand as my grandparents had just gone through it with my Uncle Mike the year before. I knew I had to start early since I would be competing with kids all across the state and the country. I began to research colleges in my sophomore year, took my PSATs and SATs early, and by the beginning of my junior year started sending away for information from the schools that offered occupational therapy.

After three weeks there were still no envelopes with my name on them. I got home from glee club practice just before dinner one night to find my grandparents sitting at the kitchen table with a stack of envelopes between them. I knew immediately they had my name on them.

"Are those for me?" I asked glancing at my grandmother.

"Yes, and we want to talk to you about them."

My grandfather seemed angry. "Sit down. We see that you've been sending off to colleges for information and we want to know why."

I was incredulous. "What do you mean?"

My grandmother nodded to my grandfather and he said clearly, "Girls don't go to college. They go to business school or finishing school, get a decent job until they meet their husband to be and get married. In your case, there is no one to pay for you to go to business school, so you'll most likely have to work for a few years to save up the money."

He looked so serious, I knew he believed what he was saying, but I was still reeling from the whole conversation. Was he really saying what I heard him saying? Were they really telling me I could not further my education beyond gaining clerical skills? Hadn't they been talking to my uncle for the last several years about how important a good education was?

My grandmother said, "So get it out of your head. We will not be filling out the paperwork for you and without that, you cannot go. That's the end of it." She stood up and threw my mail into the trash can.

All I could muster at that point was, "I see." The lump in my throat would not allow me to say anything else. My eyes were welling up. I did not want to give them the satisfaction of knowing I was crushed so I turned and headed toward my room. Their words were exploding in my head. I stayed in my room, did not eat dinner that night, and decided to write my thoughts down and let them know exactly how I felt.

I had worked so hard to be a good student, got a job after school and on weekends, participated in extracurricular activities and did everything they had asked of me up to that point. I never sassed them back and was respectful at all times. I was grateful they had given me a roof over my head, a fact they continually reminded me. They allowed me to go to the all-girls school that I had set my sights on years before. They had made it perfectly clear they were just taking care of me until I was eighteen, when, as my grandmother had put it,

"You can get the hell out. We don't care what you do after that."

I thought they really did care and that they would be proud of me for trying to make something out of myself. I poured my heart and soul into the letter, sharing all my dreams, goals, desires, and pain. I told them how much it hurt to think they did not know me at all and did not care to know me. This was all I ever wanted. Couldn't they see that? They were not aware of my accomplishments, only my failures. Did they know I was on student council? Did they know I was vice president of my class? Couldn't they see how hard I was working to buy my own clothes and pay my own way while their son, Henry, just one year older than me, had everything handed to him but didn't seem to appreciate it at all? I hardly slept that night and in the morning, left the letter on the table as I quietly slipped out the back door.

The next day, as I walked down the long gravel road that led to my grandparents' house, I noticed my Aunt Elaine's car in the driveway. Elaine was a year younger than my dad, in her early thirties and married to a schoolteacher. She was perfect in every way and never disappointed her parents. She went to finishing school, then business school. After graduation, she got a job at the chancery where she met her husband, Tim. She and my grandmother were extremely close, and whenever there was a problem, besides my grandfather, Elaine was the one my grandmother counted on most. They lived almost forty minutes away, in Clinton, Massachusetts so it was unusual for Elaine to be visiting so close to dinner time.

As I went into the house, I saw my grandmother and my aunt sternly sitting at the kitchen table and immediately knew why she was there. My letter was lying on the table between them.

"Did you read my letter?" I began, with my heart pounding in my ears.

My grandmother picked up the letter, responding, "Yes, we did and this is what we think of it," as she tore the letter to shreds and threw it in the trash.

When I watched my grandmother tear up the letter I had stayed up half the night writing, it felt as though she was discarding me. I realized in that moment, as she stood before me in the kitchen with her arms crossed, we had reached a turning point and there was no going back. I looked at my Aunt

Elaine's face for a hint of understanding and saw none.

So I quietly said, "Then, I guess I'll have to leave." I turned and headed towards my bedroom to start gathering my belongings.

She was right on my heels, "No one else is going to take you in. You have no place to go and don't even think about going to your father's house because he already knows what you've been up to and he agrees with us."

As I pulled things out of the drawers and threw them on the bed, she threatened, "You're not taking anything we paid for."

I went out to the kitchen to get a paper bag, my grandmother continued to follow me, "And you can forget about staying at Marian High because I'll be calling Father Rueger in the morning and letting him know exactly who you are and what you've done. He'll kick you out of that school so fast, your head will spin, and you'll never get into college."

I went past her with the grocery sack back into the bedroom. She and Elaine were standing behind me as I threw the clothes on the bed in to the sack. She was still threatening me but at this point, I was not listening, intent on thinking about what I needed to take with me to get through the next twenty-four hours of work and school. Since I was on foot, I needed to be able to carry whatever I was taking. I walked past them, through the den and out the front door, clutching the bag in front of me, tears streaming down my face.

My grandmother was in the doorway still threatening, "We won't be taking you back and don't bother returning for anything else. We are changing the locks on the doors. This is no longer your home!"

Looking back, I almost feel sorry for my grandmother, as she was being the best she knew how to be. She meant well, but her limited view of the world did not allow her to accept me as someone who was striving to be more than what people thought I should and could be. At the time though, quickly hurrying up the driveway, trying to get as far away from the angry threats as I could, all I could think of was how liberating it felt to be out of there. I was done trying to please people who could never be pleased.

By the time I reached the street and headed toward my part time job at Shoetown, my thoughts turned to where I would sleep that night. I knew Trisha, my longtime friend from elementary school, was scheduled to work the early shift that day. As I walked through the front door of the store, I saw George at the register. He was an extremely likeable store manager who made a boring job fun. He looked my way and somehow he knew this was no time for jokes. He told me Trisha was in the back, and I headed straight for the storeroom, not making eye contact with any of the customers. I wanted to get behind closed doors so I could figure out what I was going to do. Trisha was organizing the shelves filled with the latest shoes in stock.

When she saw the bag I was holding in my arms, she said, "You left."

I nodded and started to cry.

Without thinking twice, she put her arms around me and said, "It's okay. It's for the best, they didn't treat you very nice, Carole."

With that, I cried even more, pouring my heart out to her, recounting every word that had been exchanged. She listened, as only dear friends listen, handing me a tissue and reassuring me that I had done the right thing.

"Do you have a place to stay tonight?" she asked, knowing how impulsive I could be.

"No. I haven't gotten that far." I answered still not regretting my decision.

"I need to get back on the floor before George comes looking for me. We'll talk more later," She hugged me one more time then went through the double doors.

I looked at the clock and saw that I had to be out on the floor in ten minutes. I was still shuddering as a child does after a deep sob. I took a deep breath to try to calm myself down and went over to the sink to wash my face. I looked in the mirror at my red, swollen eyes and thought, "Where are you going to go now?" I shoved the thought to the back of my mind and put a wet paper towel over my eyes, trying to shrink the puffiness. I changed out of my school uniform into a pair of jeans and a blouse, and then I put on my work smock. A little foundation does wonders in covering up the blotchiness, I thought, as I dabbed some makeup on my face. I put on some eye shadow, a little mascara, and some lip-gloss, and I was good to go.

I spent the next few hours waiting on customers, straightening up the store, and thinking about what I would do when the store closed at nine p.m. Trisha got off at seven, and her dad was picking her up. I looked out the window and saw Mr. McGrail pull into the parking lot in a late model Chevy that had seen better days. I saw Trisha put her coat on and run out to the car before I could say good-bye.

She came back inside a moment later and said, "We'll be back to pick you up at nine."

True to her word, Trisha came back with her dad to pick me up when I finished my shift.

I got in the car and said, "Hello, Mr. McGrail. Thanks for coming back to get me,"

Flashing a kind smile, he responded, "You bet. Have you had any supper?"

I gratefully answered, "No, not yet," knowing they would make sure I did not go to bed hungry that night.

We were all quiet the rest of the way back to the McGrails' home. When we walked up the back stairs and entered the kitchen, Mrs. McGrail was waiting for us. She was a tiny thing, slightly bent over with graying hair, but was a force to be reckoned with and a woman of strong moral convictions.

"Does anyone else want a cup of tea?" Knowing it was the beverage of choice in the McGrail household, I politely answered, "I would."

Mr. McGrail was a kind man in his late fifties with silver hair that was rapidly disappearing so he wore a buzz cut. He was a little round about the middle and always wore suspenders to keep his pants up. He was short in stature but long on kindness. At five feet six inches, I towered over both of them. He and his wife had ten children of their own and had taken in countless foster children over the years. They were Irish Catholics with hearts as big as the Grand Canyon, and their house was always filled with kids, grandkids, and foster kids. They had a big kitchen table with a bench on one side and chairs on the other side. The table was always cluttered with newspapers, the kids' schoolbooks, baby items, and whatever Mrs. McGrail was working on that month. She was always collecting things to give to other people.

I sat down on the bench at the big, cluttered table, and Mrs. McGrail cleared a little space for the four of us. Once the tea was steeping, she asked,

"Would you like some leftover hidden corn casserole?"

I loved Mrs. McGrail's casserole as it was not a dish my family ever made so I did not hesitate to accept.

While the leftovers were warming in the oven, we all sat down to drink our tea and Mr. McGrail said,

"Carole, we don't know what happened today, but we do know you. We know your life hasn't been easy. You're a good kid and a good person, and we want you to know that our home is your home for as long as you need it to be."

I started to cry and through my tears said,

"Thank you, both, very much."

After supper, Trisha took me upstairs and emptied out a drawer in her dresser so that I could put my things away. We talked about where I could catch the bus in the morning and what time I should get out there. There were two bedrooms upstairs separated by a long hallway and a bathroom in the middle. Trisha's little sister, Martha, slept in the other room and was already asleep. Trisha and I would sleep in twin beds opposite one another in a room the size of a dorm room. Since we were in the attic portion of the house, the wall over Trisha's bed was sloped, but mine was not. She had switched beds so I would not be claustrophobic. I could not believe I had been so readily accepted into this family's home, while my own family made me feel that I was too much trouble.

I caught the bus to school with no problem but much to my chagrin, my grandmother Marie's brother, who worked as a bus driver for the City of Worcester was driving the bus. He was my absolute, all time, favorite uncle, and this was a tense moment. He politely said,

"Good Morning, Carole."

"Good morning, Uncle Ally." I replied as I quickly made my way past him.

He was all business that morning. He closed the doors, checked his side mirrors, put the blinker on and started to pull back out in to traffic so I headed onto the far end of the bus, slinking down in the seat so that he couldn't see me all that well. I made sure I exited via the back door and waved as I got off, feeling like I had dodged a bullet for the moment. But I knew he'd be calling my grandmother to let her know where I was. Worcester was a city of approximately seven hundred fifty thousand people at that time, but throughout my whole life, it seemed that there was always someone reporting my activities to my grandmother. She always knew what I was doing and who I was with.

Given my grandmother's threat to call the headmaster and have me expelled, I thought I should visit with Father Rueger before she had a chance to call. I waited outside his office for what seemed to be an eternity, wondering if this would be my last day with all my friends at the best school I had ever attended. The teachers truly cared about each one of us, and I was one step away from graduation. Between my part-time job after school and the money I earned waitressing on weekends, I could pay the tuition if Father Rueger would let me make monthly payments instead of paying it all up front. I did not even know if my grandmother had made any payments at all this year. The door to the headmaster's office opened and Father Rueger was standing in front of me motioning me into his office.

Thinking that most likely I would be packing up my things once the meeting was over, I plunged head long into the entire turn of events including the fact that I had run away and was now living with the McGrails. I finished with,

"I have a part time job, Father, and if you'll tell me how much I owe, I'll pay so much each month until the tuition is paid in full. Will that be okay?"

Father Rueger was typically seen walking the hallways, roaming the cafeteria during lunch periods, making sure everyone towed the line. He was a kind man, but he was the headmaster after all, and there were stories about how he put people in their place and that he occasionally showed a bit of a temper. I studied his face for a glimpse of that now. He was a fairly young headmaster, in his forties with a full head of jet black hair, a swarthy complexion, and piercing blue eyes. He was very energetic, and he seemed to be taking in many things at once. His eyes were usually scanning the room, and it was hard to tell if he was really listening to you. That's why the whole encounter was disconcerting to me because he seemed extremely focused and intent on what I had to say.

Father Rueger's response took me totally by surprise. He looked at me as if studying my face would help him decide what he was about to say. He started off with,

"I think it's interesting that your grandmother doesn't think that I can't see how involved they are with their son's education and extracurricular activities just because he goes to St. John's. I am also aware that they contribute a great deal monetarily as well, yet there is none of that on this side of the table. I don't ever remember seeing your grandparents attend one event during the entire time that you've been here."

I could not believe what I was hearing. Other people, important people like Father Rueger, could see where my grandparents' priorities really were even though they talked a big game. They were always letting me and everyone else know all that they did for me. They continually shuddered to think what would happen to me without them, since nobody else wanted me. Suddenly, I was beginning to think I had a chance of staying at Marian High until graduation.

The next words that came out totally flustered me as I heard him saying, "Carole, don't worry about losing your place here. If Marian High had just a handful of students like you, this would be a great school. Your grandmother's words will carry no weight here."

I could feel my face getting red, as I was not used to compliments and although I was close to going completely numb over what I was hearing, I forged on and asked,

"Can you tell me how much I owe in tuition, Father?"

He waved his hand as if it was inconsequential and said,

"Don't worry about the tuition, it's covered. Is there anything else I can help you with?"

I could not believe my good fortune. I stood up and felt like the weight of the world had been lifted off my shoulders.

"No Father, that's all I needed. I appreciate your help more than you know, Father."

He stood up and came around the desk, put his arm around my shoulders and gave me a slight hug while saying,

"Okay, Kiddo. Get to class before you miss the whole period and don't forget to change your address with the front office."

"Yes, Father, I will. Thanks again!" I wanted to skip down the hallway. My heart was singing and my mind was buzzing with all the thoughts of how my life had changed so drastically in the last twenty-four hours.

As I walked back to class, my thoughts were racing. I couldn't wait to tell Trisha and her parents that everything was going to be okay and I wouldn't have to transfer to public school after all. Now I could continue applying to colleges and not have to worry about who would fill out the paperwork. I spent the next few months researching schools and sending off all the required paperwork to become an emancipated minor. Taking this step would allow me to apply on my own without parental consent and without stating my parents' income.

By the end of November, I came home to find an envelope from Boston University sitting on the kitchen table. I tore it open, almost afraid to read it, and then had to re-read it several times. The words *you have been accepted* finally sank into my brain. Who would have ever believed that a kid who came from nothing, had no connections, and not a penny to her name could ever be accepted into a top-notch school like Boston University? Even the guidance counselor told me that I was not smart enough to go to a four year university and that I should lower my sights.

Now that I was living with the McGrails, I was beginning to realize that there were people who believed in me, and they were good people doing good things in the world. This realization propelled me forward. Little did I know that my whole world was about to open up.

In the spring of my senior year, I was also accepted at Tufts University and Ohio State. While the first two schools offered partial financial aid, BU offered a full academic scholarship, and that sealed the deal. The next several weeks leading up to graduation were filled with excitement, anticipation, and lots of emotion. Friends were making plans for graduation parties and after graduation trips. Since I was vice president of my class that year, I was chosen to assist in the after-graduation planning for a week at Cape Cod. There were almost thirty girls signed up to go. I was nervous when I ran it by Mr. and Mrs. McGrail, afraid they would tell me I was not allowed to go, just as my grandparents would have. Instead, after listening to my request they trustingly said,

"Carole, we'll leave that decision up to you. We trust in your judgment."

A few weeks prior to graduation, I had a dream about the trip to the Cape. I clearly saw all my friends in a cottage on the beach at a party. The word traveled quickly and the party got out of control resulting in the Massachusetts State Police being called. Drugs were found at the party and everyone present was arrested. I woke up in a cold sweat, and the more I thought about it, the more nervous I became. What if that really did end up happening? How would that affect my plans to go to college or get a decent job? Much to the anger and dismay of my close friends, I made the arrangements for everyone else to go but decided to stay home and start work immediately after graduation to save as much money as I could.

So many wonderful things were happening and one of the most memorable was when Father

Rueger called me into his office and gave me a graduation card. It contained a check for a $100 with a note that said, "I knew you could do it, Kiddo! Congratulations and here's a little something for books."

The day after graduation, all my closest friends headed for the Cape. Ten days later, I received a call that the police raided the beach house where my friends were holding a party. The police found drugs in the house, and three of my friends had been arrested on felony drug charges.

Chapter 10

Being accepted to Boston University on a full
scholarship was a huge accomplishment, and
though the scholarship covered tuition, I still needed
to figure out how I was going to cover living
expenses. I applied for a number of grants and
scholarships to assist with the additional costs. I
went to the library on a regular basis to conduct
research on which scholarships I might stand a good
chance of getting. I applied to many, some of which
were local.

One day, right before graduation, Mrs. McGrail
handed me the phone saying some woman she
didn't recognize was asking for me. I wondered
who it could be. I had never received a phone call
from anyone other than my close friends since
moving to the McGrails' home. The woman on the
other end of the line began,

"You don't know me, my name is Liz Gianelli
and I'm a member of the scholarship committee for
the Franco American club. You were in the running
for the scholarship with Sheriff Hermann's
daughter. While you did not receive the scholarship
as I believe you should have, I am calling to see if
there is something I personally might help you with,

as I truly feel you were the more deserving candidate."

I was taken aback. "I appreciate your phone call and thank you for supporting me." I didn't know what else to say.

Mrs. Gianelli continued. "I have just finished putting my own kids through college, and I know that living costs can be extremely expensive, sometimes more than the cost of tuition in a city like Boston. I wanted to tell you about an opportunity to apply for a space in a cooperative women's dormitory at BU. It's called the Harriet E. Richards coop house. It is for women of modest means who otherwise would not be able to attend BU. I'm familiar with it because I am an alumnus of the house. For a total of ninety dollars a month for room and board, the residents share the cleaning and cooking and must commit to work a few hours a month at the Boston Food Coop. I called the house president to inquire about potential vacancies for the upcoming school year. She informed me that there are currently three openings for next year, and they are accepting applications. So if you think this might be something you are interested in, I'll mail the application to you."

Interested? I had to hold myself back from jumping up and down as I quickly said,

"That sounds wonderful and I would be very interested in applying."

She went on to say, "Now, Carole, please understand that I have no control over who gets chosen and the house president did say that there is a lot of competition this year. But if you write a compelling essay, be sure and tell them about all of your accomplishments and what this would mean to you. I think you stand a good chance of getting in to the house."

After giving Mrs. Gianelli my address and thanking her profusely, I began to think about how fortunate I was and wondered why a total stranger would take such a personal interest in me. Living expenses were definitely a major consideration in order for me to attend Boston University, and I had no idea at that point in time how I would pay for food and a dorm. Within a few days, the application arrived and I took great care to fill it out completely and get it back to the committee before the deadline. Within a few weeks, I received a call from a committee member at the house asking me when I could go to Boston for a face-to-face interview with the selection panel. I called Mrs. Gianelli to share the news and she assured me that it was a good sign.

"Don't be nervous, Carole, just be yourself. You're an intelligent, well-spoken young woman, and I am sure you will impress the committee just as you impressed me."

I was at a loss for words. How could this woman, who barely knew me, see all of this in me? Why would she take the time to help me, of all people?

The morning of the interview, I caught the first city bus of the day at five thirty a.m. to take me close to downtown Worcester. I walked several blocks to the Greyhound bus station to catch the next bus to Boston for my ten a.m. interview. The

bus was filled with daily commuters who lived in
Worcester and commuted the one-hour trip every
day. As I studied their faces, I could not detect a
sense of excitement about the fact that they were on
their way to Boston, a major city and the home of
the Celtics, Bruins and the Red Sox. We were
traveling to one of the most historic cities in the
United States. Boston was so much more exciting
and alive than the boring, industrial manufacturing
city we were leaving. I was on my way to the home
of many well-known colleges and universities in the
country, a city to which I was hoping to move in the
near future. I really needed to do well in the
interview to make my dream a reality.

Once I reached the bus terminal in Boston, I
had to figure out how to take the subway to Boston
University and then to Bay State Road, where the
Harriet E. Richards house was located. As I made
my way to Boston Commons, I was awestruck by
the mixture of historical architecture and modern
office buildings, the hustle and bustle of the city,
the gold dome of the capitol, and the beauty of the
commons in the center of it all. I descended the
stairs to the green line, one of the oldest subways in
the country, and could hear the screech of the metal
wheels on the steel rails. When I reached the
platform, there were people hurrying in all
directions. Some went toward the sign marked the
Red line, which had a stop marked Harvard Square,
others went towards the Blue line, which led to

Government Center or the Orange line, which would take them to Chinatown or the famous Haymarket Square.

It was all so overwhelming, but in the middle of it all was a friendly transit worker in the familiar grey uniform inside a black wrought-iron and glass booth that was more than happy to help a young girl find her way.

"Boston University, Bay State Road? Sure! Take the green line outbound to Boston College, and get off at the Boston University stop, which is the first stop above ground after Kenmore Square. Bay State Road will be one block from your stop."

As the train came out of the tunnel and headed above ground, I saw the skyline of Boston University along Commonwealth Avenue. The train stopped right in front of an ornate granite building known as Marsh Chapel, and I quickly got off.

Just as the transit employee said, Bay State Road was just a block from the stop, and as I rounded the corner I could see the Charles River to my left and straight ahead, beautiful ivy-covered brownstones lined both sides of the street. Before I knew it, I was standing in front of the gates leading to the Harriet E. Richards coop house. A woman I had never met had shared this amazing opportunity with me, and somehow it was important to not let her down.

The house had green marble columns and a grand piano in the foyer. I was so nervous that I remember little about the interview except that it was difficult to read the faces of the girls. As I walked away, I left with no clue as to whether I would be accepted. The days and weeks passed, and just when I had begun to give up hope, a letter arrived in the mail from HER house. My heart was racing as I tore open the envelope. My eyes scanned the page, and on the third line down were the words: *You have been accepted.*

I ran upstairs to call Mrs. Gianelli. I couldn't wait to share the good news with this woman I still had not met. As soon as I heard her voice on the other end, I could hardly contain myself.

"I made it! I got accepted into HER house! I got the letter a few minutes ago and I can't thank you enough."

With the voice of a proud mother Mrs. Gianelli said, "I knew you could do it, Carole. Congratulations! Now, do you have a ride to school, because if not, I'd love to take you?"

So we made plans to depart for BU and HER house just one week shy of my eighteenth birthday. Between working full time and saying good-bye to high school friends, the next few weeks were filled with shopping for bedding, toiletries, and supplies to get me through the first few months of school in. Of my closest friends, only one was leaving Worcester. Trish was going to Fitchburg State to study medical technology. The rest were going to study locally or work for a while. But one thing was certain: we would never recapture the closeness we currently felt as our lives were now taking different paths.

News of my acceptance and scholarship made it to the local newspaper right before my 18th birthday. Surprisingly, both my mother's and my father's sides of the family invited me to an early birthday dinner on the same day. I visited my dad's family briefly, letting them know I could not stay for dinner. My dad hadn't made it home yet, so the only one there was Mary. We sat at the kitchen table for a bit, she asked me about my plans for school. When I told her I couldn't wait any longer as I was late for dinner at my maternal grandmother's house, she gave me a gift and wished me well. It was strained at best.

I drove directly to my maternal grandmother's home for dinner. My grandparents and my mother's sister had prepared a nice birthday dinner and purchased a trunk full of toiletries, towels, and sheets as a send-off for college. Their kindness and generosity meant so much and, while relations had been very strained, the gesture made me realize they were proud of my accomplishments.

I approached my grandmother after dinner to thank her privately. Within a few minutes the conversation took a different turn when she looked at me and said,

"I still don't understand why you went to live with your father's side of the family. Why didn't you call me? Do you know how much that hurt me?"

Was she kidding? I looked at her, not believing that she had totally blocked out the memory of me calling her from the phone booth, begging her to help me.

"But I did call you, Gram. You told me things weren't that bad."

"Why are you making things up, Carole Jane? Don't you think I would have done something if I had known how bad it was?"

For years to come, my grandmother would remind me of the pain my choices had cost her. I would listen and apologize each time.

The day had finally arrived when Mrs. Gianelli was knocking on the door and strangely enough, when we met, I felt I had known her forever. The ride to Boston was over before I knew it, and Mrs. G. was closing the trunk of her car. All up and down Bay State Road, students were unloading cars while others were helping to carry things into the dorms. When I turned around there were students offering to carry my things into HER house, too. I gratefully hugged Mrs. G., thinking no words could express my gratitude to this stranger who came into my life to help me with exactly what I needed when I needed it.

The next several weeks were like a whirlwind of activity, meeting new roommates, waiting in line to register for classes, buying books, and finding classrooms on a campus that was thirteen miles long. Back then there were no orientations; you were left to figure it out on your own. Soon I was settling into a routine of work, study, classes and activities at the house.

I only saw Mrs. G. one more time during my first year at BU. She had stopped by the dorm on her way to visit relatives and wanted to leave me a card and a roll of quarters. She was sure I would need them to do my laundry, and how right she was. As I hugged her, I had a feeling it might be our last time to see each other, but her kindness and generosity had connected us forever.

Chapter 11

College was much harder than I ever imagined and there was no margin for error. I had chosen my field of study based on an experience in one of the elementary schools I attended that was divided into two wings. One wing was for disabled children and provided full therapeutic services in addition to the classroom curriculum. There was an audiology and speech department, a physical and occupational therapy department, a fully staffed clinic with a nutritionist on staff. The daily contact with these children taught me many lessons and filled me with a desire to make a difference. In particular, I had the chance to shadow the occupational therapist that inspired me to study that field. Back then, Occupational Therapy, (OT) was a fairly obscure profession, and most people would ask, "What's that?" My baby sister used to tell people I was going to be an occupied terrorist. I enjoyed telling people about my dream; it was different and interesting. It sounded professional and people seemed to be impressed by it.

Winning a full scholarship to Boston University and getting accepted in to the Harriett E. Richards house was only half the battle to fulfilling my dream of being the first college graduate in my immediate family. The other half was staying there. In the fall of my junior year of college, I sustained a third-degree burn on my leg. I was sick to my stomach and blacked out while in the bathroom. When I woke up on the floor, my leg was up against the radiator. For several days, I continued to work and go to class, but the pain was excruciating and after finishing my mid-term exams, I took a taxi to the emergency room. There was no way I could walk to the nearest corner, let alone the two miles to Beth Israel Hospital.

When I got to the Emergency Room, a nurse, never taking her eyes away from the forms in front of her, asked, "What are you here for?"

"I burned my leg a few weeks ago and the pain is worsening. I was hoping someone could look at it?" She looked up and handed me a clipboard with lots of forms on it.

"Fill these out and bring them back. When you're done, take a seat."

More than an hour went by when finally a male voice called my name,

"Carole?"

I looked toward the voice and saw an older man in a white coat with a stethoscope around his neck. His hair was black with flecks of silver throughout.

"I'm Doctor Reardon," he said as he sat down at the desk. "What seems to be the problem today?"

Sitting down in the chair next to his desk I said, "Well, Doctor, I burned my leg about two weeks ago and the pain is excruciating. I went to the BU student clinic, and they gave me some pain pills and told me to keep it clean. I tried taking the pills, but they were so strong I couldn't study for mid-terms. The pain seems to be getting worse, and I was wondering if you could take a look at it?"

Looking over the rim of his reading glasses, he said, "Why don't you roll up your pant leg and let me see what we're talking about?" He took one look and said, "Holy Mother of God!" Calling the nurse to bring me a wheel chair, he said, "You're being admitted immediately so if you have anyone you need to call, call them now."

The first skin graft was done with pig skin and after almost two weeks was deemed a failure. Doctor Reardon insisted on doing a second skin graft, this time taking skin from my right thigh. The whole time I was in the hospital, my roommate, Marie, who was also an OT student, brought me assignments almost every day, or she would call me with the reading assignments. After another ten days in the hospital, the second graft was also pronounced a failure. Doctor Reardon scheduled a third surgery but I insisted we do it over Christmas break so that I could finish the semester and take my final exams. He was fine with that. I worked hard to make up the work I had missed and I took all my final exams.

I was admitted back into Beth Israel a few days before Christmas and once again, they took skin from the top of my other thigh. It was pretty lonely this time around since everyone had gone home for the holidays. But if the graft took, it would be worth it.

The loneliness and fear of yet a third surgery made me pick up the phone against my better judgment and dial my dad's number. I remember hesitating a little when I heard his voice answer the phone, but I forged on in hopes that he missed me as I much as I missed him. I said,

"Hi Dad, it's me, Carole." I paused and heard the longest silence coming from the other end.

Finally he said, "Yeah, what do you want?"

I immediately regretted dialing the number but there was no going back now, he was on the other end of the line so I continued.

"I just wanted to call you and wish you a Merry Christmas, Dad. I have been thinking about you. Are you okay?"

He responded with what sounded like disinterest in his voice, "I'm fine."

I thought well, you've come this far so you might as well go all the way and I said,

"I'm not going to be able to make it to Worcester for the holidays this year."

"Oh, yeah?" I could tell he wasn't the least bit interested so I laid it all out.

"Yeah, I'm at Beth Israel hospital in Brookline. I'm scheduled to have a skin graft tomorrow for a burn on my leg."

With little emotion, he said, "That's too bad." And there it was: the door was shut.

On January 2, Doctor Reardon came in to pull off the bandages. I could tell by the look on his face that once again, the graft did not take.

"The area where the burn is located has a poor blood supply, which gives it a greater chance for infection. I'd like to try again, but I understand you need to get back to school in time for the start of the semester. So I'm going to release you with a few prescriptions, and the nurse will go over how to care for the wound until it heals, which could take up to a year. You will need to schedule a follow-up appointment at my office, and we'll keep an eye on you until this heals. I wish I had better news for you, Carole, but we gave it our best shot."

As I walked home from the hospital, I felt like I had been on a roller coaster for the last three months. I didn't understand why I had to go through three failed surgeries. The only difference was that my status at BU was now in jeopardy because of all the missed classes. It took more than a year, but eventually the area around the burn healed on its own.

By May, one week before final exams, I was called into the Dean of Allied Health's office. I had never even met the dean and had no idea why I was being summoned. To this day, I do not even remember the woman's face, just the conversation. The dean had the unpleasant task of informing me that one of my professors decided to challenge whether credit should be given to me since I had not physically attended all her classes. Even though I had made up all the course work and maintained an *A* average, the professor insisted I could not have benefited from her class, so she decided to bring it before an academic review team of five individuals. Interestingly, my professor was a member of the team and her vote was already cast. The dean informed me that they had voted 3–2 not to award me credit for the course, which meant that the subsequent course I had taken in the spring semester did not count either. There was no opportunity to appeal. The decision was final.

Upon hearing those devastating words, everything else became a blur. Somehow I stumbled through the campus, made my way across bustling Commonwealth Avenue in Boston during rush hour with trolleys rumbling in both directions. I do not recall hearing a sound. My world had crumbled down around me. What was I going to do now? The scholarship would not wait for me to make up the course work. How would I survive? Where would I go? Without the scholarship, I could not pay my rent. There was no turning back but there was no going forward.

Chapter 12

Soon the bills started piling up, and with no scholarship money or earnings from work-study coming in to help with rent and utilities. I had to find work quickly. In Boston, it's hard to find a decent-paying job when you are competing with thousands of college grads. Eventually, I came to the realization that I had to accept whatever would help me keep a roof over my head.

So with a two-hundred-dollar loan from my credit card to purchased inventory, a week after dropping out of school, I got a job driving an ice cream truck. I had to buy the ice cream up front and pay a daily rental fee for the use of the truck plus gas. I was not familiar with the suburbs surrounding the Boston area, so I had a bit of a learning curve. I was working ten to twelve hours a day, nights, and weekends, and dealing with brutal competition. After two months of spending most of my profits on gas, truck-rental fees, and inventory, I realized I was not going to make ends meet. Thus, I began working a string of minimum wage jobs.

I took on two more roommates to lower my expenses and worked a full time job in an optical/dental office during the day. All the while I kept looking for something in social services that would allow me an opportunity to go back to school to finish my degree. Trying to make ends meet in Boston was like watching salmon swim upstream. I eventually had to let my apartment go and became homeless. After spending a few nights in my car, a friend let me stay on her couch for several weeks.

After a year of searching, I was finally hired as a Mental Health Assistant with the Massachusetts Department of Mental Health. I started at the Walter E. Fernald State Hospital in Waltham. Within six months, I was promoted to an occupational therapy assistant. At night I worked in a booth in the local mall engraving and making keys. But by 1979, I was facing eviction once again after my roommate moved out while I was at work, leaving me with all the utility bills and unpaid rent.

I just could not get ahead. The cost of living in Boston was more than I could handle earning a little more than $14,000 a year. I had to quit my jobs and move back to Worcester. The McGrails were gracious enough to open their door to me once again.

Chapter 13

When I first started working at the Department of Mental Health, I was hoping to find a job that would help me get ahead. I had just moved back to Worcester after living in Boston for five years. I had lost all my contacts and felt like I was starting all over again. I was referred to the Glavin Regional Center in Shrewsbury by the local employment commission. It seemed they had an opening for a mental health aide. I learned that I would be working with profoundly mentally disabled adolescents. With my background in Occupational Therapy and mental health, I felt as though I could do a good job and make a difference for the residents while representing the department well.

It seemed like everyone I met at Glavin on the night shift was stuck in a rut. They worked to make ends meet and went to the Irish club after work. No one was happy with their job or felt good about the work they did. It was always a means to an end, a way to pay the bills and keep a roof over your head. If you stuck with it long enough and were content with the status quo, you could eventually retire from the same job. Was that all there was to life? I felt like there had to be more. I wanted more for myself. I wanted to feel fulfilled by my work. I wanted to do something life-changing both for myself and for others.

After a few months, I was promoted to evening supervisor. It felt good to know that the administration trusted me at a young age with such a great deal of responsibility. I supervised two units that housed twenty residents. Some were physically disabled as well. Some of the children were born without defects and had become disabled due to severe physical and emotional abuse. It was heartbreaking to learn their stories, and in a short period of time, I got to know them well and developed a deep sense of caring for them. I could read their behavior and knew when it was escalating, which was critical to avoid accidents or injuries. The most difficult periods were when they were taken off their medication, as required by law at least once a year. Many of the residents became dangerous to themselves and to others. Half of the residents were in a locked ward due to their unpredictable behavior. That's where I started. I guess they put you in the most difficult jobs first as a weeding-out process. It was advantageous for me to be able to navigate the behavioral roller coaster the residents had us on in order to keep them safe and to keep ourselves safe.

Over time, the goal was to assist the residents to improve their ability to care for themselves by working on activities of daily living skills and modifying behavior. But it seemed like we would take one step forward and two steps back. Changes in staffing and medication were always triggers. We were all aware of the challenges and we were trained to deal with behavioral changes. Experienced workers confronted irrational behavior on a daily basis. That's why, an incident that took place not once but twice over a period of two weeks was especially difficult to understand.

I came around the corner one evening and witnessed a tenured employee slapping a profoundly disabled resident in the face. When I asked her to leave the area, she told me the patient had spit in her face, and she reacted without thinking. After a counseling session in which the worker displayed extreme remorse, I decided not to press charges. A few weeks later, the same worker was threatening to burn the same client with a lit cigarette.

I dismissed the worker immediately and filed charges. Unfortunately, her father was the union representative for our facility. I was ostracized, taunted, and harassed for the length of the investigation that dragged on for more than nine months. In the end, the state attorney chose not to file charges because the worker was single and had become pregnant after the incident had occurred.

As much as I loved the kids I was charged to protect, the bureaucracy in place at the time made me feel powerless to do my job. I decided to move on, knowing that one day, if I was ever in a position to make the rules, they would be in favor of what was right and just, no matter how difficult. This was by far, one of the hardest lessons I was forced to learn as an adult. I resigned the same day and began making plans to work overseas. I sold what I could and left the rest with a friend. My foster family was dead set against my decision, but my friends and acquaintances thought it was cool.

I knew there had to be more to life than working and going out for a beer afterward. I wanted to make a difference in the world, and I wanted to learn more about myself. As I sat on the plane headed to Bangkok, listening to the drone of the engines, I wondered what my new life would hold for me. Where would I live and work? I was excited about learning a new language, a new culture, eating different food, and seeing new places. I had spent my entire life in one state. It was time to see the world, to grow up, and to leave everything I knew behind. It was time to find out who I could be, without the negative influences that had plagued me for so long. Little did I know, when I left Massachusetts a few days later, my life was about to change and morph in so many different ways over the next several decades. Even though I never lived in Massachusetts again, the lessons I learned and the people who taught them to me played a huge role in making me the person I am today.

Chapter 14

In 1980, the year I quit my job with the Massachusetts Department of Mental Health and went to Thailand, post-Vietnam America was fixated on Phil Donahue. Oprah was becoming a household word, Jimmy Carter was president, and the country was going through a horrible recession with interest rates hovering around sixteen and a half per cent. The American dream of home ownership seemed highly unattainable to me in my early twenties, and the country was still smarting from the failed hostage rescue attempts in Iran. At the age of twenty-three, I wanted something more in my life. I wanted my life to have meaning.

I decided to travel to Thailand as a starting point for my overseas journey because one of the McGrails' daughters, Teresa, was living two hours south of Bangkok with her husband Paul and their two little boys. Paul was from Petchburi, Thailand, and had been called back to run the family business. Before they moved to Thailand, I had grown close to Teresa while I was in college and had often spent weekends at her home. I babysat her little boys and missed her dearly.

Thailand is bordered by Myanmar, Laos, Vietnam, Cambodia, and Malaysia. Due to the unrest in Southeast Asia, with the exception of Malaysia, there were refugee camps all along the Thai borders. Teresa and Paul graciously offered me a place to stay until I got a position teaching English as a second language (ESL). I hoped to be able to find a job either teaching in a small village or in one of the camps.

Shortly after arriving in Thailand, I was hired by Save the Children to teach English on the Thai-Lao border in a refugee camp for Laotian hill tribe refugees, called the Hmong. All the international aid workers, about sixty in number, lived in the tiny Thai village of Chiang Khan. They traveled by van or songthaews to camp Ban Vinai which was an hour away. Songthaews are pickup trucks with covered beds and two benches for transporting people.

Chiang Khan was a small sleepy village on the Mekong River, with a few shops run by Chinese merchants on the main drag and one hotel on the river across from Laos where *farang*, or Westerners, stayed when passing through. Most of the houses were made of wood with tin roofs. Many of the houses on the main street along the river were all connected with businesses run out of the front part of the house. The living quarters were upstairs or in the back of the house. The influx of international aid workers had created a demand for housing and foreign goods such as bread, butter, milk, and cheese, among many other western goods. It seemed our presence was good for the local economy.

The day after we arrived in Chiang Kahn, we were picked up by a songthaew hired specifically for Save the Children teachers. The ride to the camp was along a red, dusty road that wound its way along the river's edge in places. We passed rice fields where local farmers were making their way to the fields with their water buffalo in tow. A little further up the road we passed a local *wat*, or temple, and saw a group of monks in saffron robes walking single file, most likely on their way to get the daily offering of sticky rice and fish from the local villagers. The road was bumpy in places and the dust billowed up in clouds behind the truck as we made our way down the winding road. When we passed the occasional vehicle coming in the opposite direction, we were enveloped in the same red dust that covered the leaves on the trees and vines that lined the road.

Ban Vinai was by far, the largest refugee camp in Thailand, with a population of more than 14,000 Hmong in 1980. The Hmong people were fierce fighters, hard working, and very loyal. They were U.S. allies in the resistance against the Pathet Lao regime during the takeover of Laos. When Laos fell in 1975, thousands of Hmong along with their leader, General Vang Pao, were evacuated to the United States. Unfortunately thousands more remained in the hills of Laos and were on the run for several years after the fall.

The Hmong were a trusting people and in particular trusted and followed the direction of their leader. Vang Pao was now telling them not to sign up to go on to a third country like the United States but to stay and train so they could take Laos back. The camp population was growing steadily as more Hmong escaped in the middle of the night across the Mekong River. They carried their belongings on their backs, staying afloat with bamboo logs. The strong river current would eventually wash them up on the banks of Thailand—if they weren't shot midstream.

On my first day, the truck dropped five of us off at the Save the Children office in the camp. We were given a book, some chalk, an eraser, and someone to take us to our assigned classrooms. That was the extent of our training. As we walked through the camp toward the classroom area, I observed open-air markets where the Hmong sold beautiful hand-embroidered items, among many other things. I also noted various aid groups in charge of different basic needs for the camp residents. World Vision provided water and drainage systems in the camp and ran the hospital. The Catholic Office of Emergency Refugee Relief (COERR) was responsible for the leprosy unit. They provided training and education to the family members and later built a rehab clinic for the entire camp. Save the Children provided ESL classes, and the International Rescue Committee (IRC) was responsible for bulk food and water distribution. There were smaller groups that came and went during my time at Ban Vinai, but World Vision, COERR, Save the Children and the IRC were the major players in 1980.

For the first three months, I worked with Save the Children until they terminated their program and moved to Bangkok. I had been volunteering to help the sisters with COERR to survey the needs of the camp on the weekends. When they heard Save the Children was leaving, they offered me a full-time position to assist them with building the rehabilitation clinic in the camp.

My first classroom at Ban Vanai was an open-air classroom with no walls, a tin roof, and a cement floor. The slabs were poured to allow for four back-to-back classrooms. There were three rows of classrooms all side by side. The only thing that separated one classroom from another was the freestanding blackboard. There was quite a bit of distraction when all the classrooms were full, but occasionally we would have fun by having pronunciation wars. My last class of the morning was just across from Steve Cohen's, a thirty-two-year-old teacher from Long Island. I could hear Steve telling his class to repeat after him and the next thing I heard were more than forty Hmong hill tribe refugees mimicking in unison, "The party starts at eight o'clock" in a strong Long Island accent.

Of course, I had to teach my students the correct pronunciation, so as soon as his class stopped reciting, my class repeated the same sentence after me in a perfect New England accent.

That prompted Vang Vu, one of my teenage students, to ask, "Teacher, why Mr. Steve sound different?" which led to an entire lesson on regional accents. The students were eager to learn everything and anything we had to share with them.

The Hmong were used to living off the land. They made everything by hand, from hunting knives to the huts they lived in with the exception of their radios and watches. Their living quarters were simple and their lives had revolved around hunting and farming. They strongly believe their lives are directly tied to the spirit world. This belief often conflicts with the Western world view, as was apparent one day in my classroom.

As part of the lesson, I decided to show my students pictures of skyscrapers and ask,

"Class, how would you get to the top floor of this building that has one hundred floors?"

Eager to respond, Pao Xiang, a thirteen-year-old boy sitting in the front row said,

"Have a plane drop you on the roof, Teacher?"

Tua Vo, a young girl in the third row, raised her hand and offered,

"Walk up the stairs, Teacher," convinced she must be right.

I nodded and then asked,

"How many times a day could you go up and down one hundred flights of stairs with children, the elderly, food, or other items?"

When they finally gave up, I arranged the desks to form a small three sided room. I hung two pieces of material from the ceiling in front of the room. I wrote the word *elevator* and put a picture of an elevator on the blackboard. I parted the curtains and invited them to step into the room.

Then I stepped in and reached up to close the curtains when all of a sudden an older man refused to stay in the makeshift room. He pushed his way out saying something I didn't understand.

When I asked what was wrong, Pao Xiang explained, "Hmong people believe shadow must be able to follow you. When it can't, you die."

As the weeks turned into months, I gained much respect for these resilient, hard-working people who always had a smile and were ready to help with whatever needed to be done. Even though the camp was crowded and they could no longer hunt and farm in the same ways as before, they adapted and waited for instructions from their leader, Vang Pao. News of the Hmong who had gone to the United States in 1975 arrived via missionaries from Minnesota and California, who told of young Hmong men in their twenties dying in their sleep. The transition from their roles in the familiar world of the Hmong villages to their new life in the United States was too stressful. Others were arrested for shooting squirrels in the park and for practicing polygamy. Somehow, before sending them to the United States, we needed to do more to help this group of refugees who had lost their way of life.

The rainy season in northern Thailand occasionally interrupted our daily routine. Once, one of the bridges that led to the camp washed out while we were teaching. We were forced to stay in the camp until the bridge was repaired. Five of us were assigned a ten-foot-by-eight-foot room in one of the shelters that had been built for the refugees. There were bamboo mats on the floor and someone got us a few blankets. We dropped off our books and teaching supplies and all headed over to the camp restaurant for dinner.

The main gathering place for Westerners was a thatched roof hut with bamboo tables and wooden benches with the ever-present Coca Cola sign in Thai displayed on the bamboo wall. The menu consisted of ramen noodle soup with bean curd and Hmong greens, chicken vegetable stir fry on rice, beef stir fry on rice, fried egg on rice, and various fish and vegetable dishes all served with an occasional dead fly. There was a standing joke about the newly arrived refugee worker who found a fly in his food and promptly threw it out. Three months later, he found another fly in his food, threw the fly away and kept on eating. Six months later, he again found a fly in his food and just kept eating, fly and all.

After dinner, darkness came quickly. With no electricity in the camp, all you could see were flashlights, camp fires, and every now and then a candle flickering through an open window or door as you passed by huts and shelters. You could hear the occasional cry from a baby, someone playing a Hmong flute, and families settling in for the night. It seemed that the camp was winding down early or so I thought.

For some reason, I glanced toward the classroom area expecting to see total darkness and was surprised to see light glowing through the cracks of the shuttered windows. I thought it strange that anyone would be teaching so late at night and decided to walk over to see what kind of class was being taught. As I came closer to the window, I heard what sounded like a two-way radio with an American male voice speaking. Next, I heard a Hmong male voice speaking English saying, "Roger. We have no visual at this time. Need new coordinates. Over." I peered through the cracks and was surprised to see two of my teenage students among the group of men.

I returned to the room and said nothing to the other teachers. I really wasn't sure what I had seen and heard. A few weeks later, one of the students I had seen through the cracks, Vu Tang, joined me for a soda on the bench near my classroom.

He asked, "Why did you come to Ban Vinai?"

I answered without really thinking, "I wanted to help in some way."

Genuinely curious, he went on, "Why would you want to leave a good life in America to live like us?"

I guess it made little sense to someone in his position, and in that moment I said what I had never acknowledged before:

"Because I know I have been given more than most just because I was born in America. I was given the right to an education, shelter, food, and medicine. I have the right to vote and practice whatever religion I choose. I want to help you get those things too, if that's what you want."

He thought for a bit, and then asked, "Do you think I should go to America or should I stay here and try to go back to Laos?"

Remembering that night a few weeks back, I asked, "Do you think you can go back safely?"

He then told me, "I have gone back many times to help my family still living in Laos. It is not safe for Hmong to live, but they are afraid to leave village. They wait for America to send supplies."

Confused, I asked, "Why would they wait for America to send supplies?"

Without hesitation, he answered, "American CIA send planes at night, drop supplies. With supplies, we fight, get Laos back."

It had been five years since the official end of the Vietnam War, why would the Hmong think they still had a chance to remove the Pathet Lao regime from power?

At this point many had been in the camp since the fall of Laos, and a new generation of Hmong was growing up in Ban Vinai. Many were abandoning the traditional Hmong dress for western clothing or, in the case of the women, Thai sarongs and western shirts. Although they still celebrated the Hmong New Year in traditional style, carried on the traditional ball-tossing courtship rituals, and called on the local shaman as their spiritual healer. Some would take advantage of western medicine as well by going to the hospital in the camp but only as a last resort.

Chapter 15

When word of my background in Occupational Therapy reached one of the sisters that served with Catholic Overseas Emergency Refugee and Relief (COERR), I was asked to volunteer on the weekends to help survey the rehabilitation needs of the camp inhabitants. COERR wanted to build a rehabilitation clinic in the camp and needed the data to obtain funding. Helping the sisters reach their goals was a priceless experience and one that I learned a great deal from.

When Save the Children left Ban Vinai, I transitioned over to working with COERR full time. I worked with three Daughters of Charity Catholic sisters from the Philippines. Sister Adelita was a nurse in charge of the leprosy unit, Sister Teresita was responsible for the rehab clinic and Sister Pierre Marie Bail oversaw the operations from Chiang Khan. I began attending the weekly hospital meetings since the rehab clinic was located in the hospital compound. The head of the hospital was a young Filipino doctor, Doctor Santos, and he usually conducted the meetings.

At the first meeting I attended, Doctor Santos was sharing reports about illnesses in the camp that week, which included malaria, tuberculosis, shigellosis, giardia, malnourishment, asthma, and, worst of all, secondary pneumonia resulting from babies with tetanus. The Hmong delivered their babies at home and cut the umbilical cords with unsterile hunting knives. The newborn mortality rate was 50 percent in the camp as the infants died from secondary pneumonia. As I listened, I wondered what treatments were being given for pneumonia but was afraid to inquire in front of the entire group since I did not feel qualified to ask.

After the meeting, I went to the medical chief who was turning towards the door, "Dr. Santos, may I ask you a question about the infants with secondary pneumonia?"

He seemed genuinely open when he turned to look at me. Encouraged, I continued, "Is anyone performing manual respiratory therapy on the infants during their stay?"

He seemed confused, "What do you mean by that?"

I demonstrated the technique by cupping my hands and explaining, "You cup your hands and gently tap the patient's lungs while they are lying on their stomach for fifteen minutes at a time. The tapping helps to stimulate the lungs and makes the patient cough. Over time, this keeps the lungs clear during their hospital stay."

Doctor Santos was intrigued now. "Well, that makes sense, I've never seen it, but it can't hurt. Do you know how to administer the therapy?"

I eagerly explained, "I was trained earlier this year when an asthmatic patient of mine was admitted to the intensive care unit. She was severely mentally disabled, nonverbal and needed one-on-one care. So we were trained to administer the therapy since the patient was frightened by the hospital personnel."

He grabbed his clip board and headed for the door saying, "Good, then it's yours."

I wasted no time in communicating our new assignment to Sister Teresita who had already been assigned four Hmong trainees from the leprosy unit earlier that week. No one in the camp would hire the family members of the lepers.

My first task was to teach them English, then train them in various occupational therapy (OT) techniques. In the United States, no one would hire me to work as an OT with only three years of college, and they would never ask an OT to perform respiratory therapy without being a certified respiratory therapist. But in this environment, all willing hands were welcome if no medication was being administered as part of the treatment.

I was eager to get started. So after demonstrating and practicing the technique with my trainees, we went to the pediatric ICU ward and identified all the tetanus babies. The hospital had cement floors, wooden walls, and open windows that were shuttered during inclement weather. There were four infants that first week, so I asked one of my assistants to explain to the mothers why we were there and that I was going to gently massage the baby's lungs. The first mother smiled and nodded okay and moved over to make room for me on the bamboo mat that covered the wooden bed.

The infant lay perfectly still with his eyes closed. I later learned this was characteristic of tetanus babies, and the lack of movement is what brought on the secondary pneumonia. I sat down on the edge of the cot and gently picked up the infant to lay him across my lap. I turned the baby's head to one side and rhythmically moved my cupped hands up and down, gently drumming the baby's lungs for fifteen minutes. We then moved to each one of the babies and performed the same technique. We made our rounds three times a day, and it became one more thing incorporated into our day. It was by far the most enjoyable task. The young mothers always seemed so happy to see us, and the babies were so tiny and helpless. I sometimes wondered if they could feel how much we wanted them to live and hoped their tiny bodies could somehow overcome this terrible start in life.

Chapter 16

Between English classes, training the workers, therapy sessions, meetings, and visits from other organizations that came to assist us with our work, my days in the camp were full. One such group came from another camp along the border with Cambodia to help us build canes, walkers, and prosthetic limbs out of bamboo and leather. Sister Teresita was always making connections wherever she could to bring in the expertise to help those disabled by war, disease, malnutrition, and birth defects.

I had been in Thailand for nearly nine months, and my visa was going to expire. The sisters assured me that COERR's administrative office in Bangkok would help me with the renewal, so I hopped on a bus to Bangkok thinking the entire process would take a few days. I met with a kind Filipino gentleman, Mr. Banayat, who was in charge of legal affairs for COERR. He explained that the process was quite simple. I just needed to fill out some paperwork and leave it with him. Then I needed to board a train to Malaysia, go to the island of Penang and in a few days check for a letter from him at the main post office. I could then return to Thailand with my new visa. It all sounded iffy at best, but Mr. Banayat worked for COERR and he appeared to be a genuinely nice man so I did as he instructed.

The next morning I took a taxi to Hualamphong Station and climbed aboard a south bound train for Kuala Lumpur, Malaysia, which was an interesting experience since the only trains I had ever boarded were Amtrak commuter trains between Boston and New York. The journey to Kuala Lumpur was a forty-eight hour trip, but I didn't need to travel that far. I only needed to cross over the border to Butterworth then take a ferry to the island of Penang, which should take a little more than twenty-four hours.

The train was actually quite comfortable, with wide leather seats for two that were opposite one another. The wide picture windows allowed for a fabulous view of the Thai countryside. The Thai landscape changed dramatically once we left the clamoring streets of Bangkok and made our way south. The further along we went, the more dramatic the north-south mountain ranges became, with lush tropical vegetation, rice fields, and the rain forest in the foreground. Thailand was truly a paradise on earth inhabited by people who were gentle, accepting, and gracious as evidenced by the commonly used phrase, *mai pen rai*, which means "it doesn't matter" or "it's okay." The Thai philosophy was one of flexibility above all else.

As I looked around the train, I saw Thai and Malaysian families and a few Westerners whom I later met in the dining car. There was a young

Canadian in his early twenties by the name of Clark, a British girl named Vickie, and Georgina was Australian, both in their early twenties as well. Clark was taking a year off from college to travel around Asia and was on his way to Borneo. They invited me to join them for a Singha beer.

Vickie was headed for Sri Lanka, and Georgina was taking the slow route back to Australia via Penang, Singapore, Jakarta, and Bali. All three had taught ESL during their travels as a means to earn a living and keep traveling, but none had worked with refugees or stayed in any one place for more than two months. Both Georgina and Vickie had been to Penang before and offered to help me find a safe, affordable hotel. They provided tips on what to see and do during my brief stay.

The time passed quickly, and it wasn't long before the train crew started converting the seating areas into sleepers. The trains from Bangkok to Malaysia were all second class sleepers and, surprisingly, they were very clean and quite comfortable. The rhythm of the train rolling along the tracks was so soothing. I actually slept quite well once I got used to the idea that I was sleeping just a few feet from several hundred strangers, and we were only separated by a curtain.

The train pulled into Butterworth, Malaysia, around mid-afternoon a little more than twenty-four hours after departing from Bangkok. Clark had already made reservations at a hotel in Butterworth so the three of us headed toward the ferry for the island of Penang. After we checked into a modest

Chinese hotel on Chulia Street, we agreed to meet in fifteen minutes to go out for dinner. Georgina was waiting by the front door when I came down the stairs.

"There's a great place called the Hong Kong Bar that I went to the last time I was here. The food is great, reasonably priced, and they speak English. What do you think?"

Before I could answer, Vickie came up from behind saying, "Hey there's a great place called the Hong Kong Bar, and it's within walking distance, what do you think?"

Georgina and I just laughed, "Sounds like we need to go to the Hong Kong Bar!"

Penang was a lovely mix of both Chinese and Muslim cultures and there were lots of shops, pubs, and restaurants with a lively tourist population and a noticeable Australian military presence. The Hong Kong Bar just happened to be right down the street from the hotel, and we were there in just a few minutes. It was full for a weekday evening, but there were still a few tables available, and we grabbed the first one we saw. The walls were lined with photos and memorabilia. The music coming from the juke box was mid-seventies American pop music, and the menu had a variety of Western and Chinese dishes to choose from with extremely reasonable prices.

Rosie a young energetic Chinese woman who appeared to be in her mid-thirties greeted us. "Hallo! You know what you like to drink?" Georgina and Vickie both answered,

"I'll have a Tiger beer." Guessing that Tiger beer was to Malaysia as Singha beer was to Thailand, I decided to join my two new found friends.

Rosie promptly came back with our drinks and had a camera with her as well. "Your first time here, right?" We all nodded. "It's customary to take your photo to hang on the wall with all the other guests that come to the Hong Kong Bar."

While she was taking our pictures, the guys at the next table began to give Rosie a hard time, "Hey, you didn't take our pictures. How come you're taking theirs?"

Without hesitation, Rosie shot back, "You're too ugly; don't want camera to break." The table erupted with raucous laughter, and we got a kick out of it too.

When the guys saw they had successfully gotten our attention, the jokes really began to fly back and forth, especially because Georgina could keep up with them. It wasn't long before they were making room for us at their table. They were all stationed at the Australian Royal Air Force Base at Butterworth and it was obvious, even through their laughter, they were homesick and really enjoyed our company. We were a willing audience and I soon became the butt of their jokes since I was the Yank and struggled to get most of the punch lines. I usually never understood what they were saying. A typical joke would go like this:

"Three blokes were working on a high-rise building project, Macca, Chook, and Simmo. Chook falls off and is killed instantly. As the ambulance takes the body away, Simmo says,

'Someone should go and tell his wife.'

Macca says, 'OK, I'm pretty good at that sensitive stuff, I'll do it.' Two hours later, Macca comes back carrying a slab of VB.

Simmo says, 'Where did you get that, Macca?'

'Chook's missus gave it to me.'

'That's unbelievable, you told the lady her husband was dead and she gave you a slab?'

Macca says, 'Well not exactly. When she answered the door, I said to her, "You must be Chook's widow."

She said, "No, I'm not a widow."

And I said, "Wanna bet me a slab?"'

Everyone would be in hysterics except me. The goal then became to expand the Yank's Australian vocabulary. We had so much fun and hated to leave, but it was late and the trip had really worn us out. The guys insisted on walking us back to our hotel. There were no protests on my end since it was later than I'd ever stayed out by myself in a strange city. So off we went with our Australian guard of eight burly soldiers who made us promise to be back at the Hong Kong (HK) Bar by seven o'clock the next night.

The next day, the three of us met for breakfast, which consisted of kopi-o kau, the best coffee ever and a delightful array of bread. My favorite bread was Roti Taiwan. This delightful sweet bread was topped with a creamy layer of some kind of peanut butter spread and nuts. They also served succulent plates of tropical fruit and the best French toast I've ever had sprinkled with sugar. In stark contrast to my daily routine in Chiang Khan, where I never ate before noon, breakfast became my favorite meal of the day.

I spent the first few days exploring the island shops, visiting historical landmarks, and learning as much as I could about the rich culture and history of Malaysia. It was so close yet very different from Thailand, but just as fascinating. Initially, all three of us would explore together, and we'd end up at the HK Bar for our daily dose of fun and laughter with the guys from RAFB Butterworth. While there were always two or three in the group that we would have already met, there were just as many new airmen we didn't know. It seemed the word was getting out about the new audience at the HK Bar.

Vickie was the first to move onto the next phase of her trip, leaving Georgina and me to really get to know one another over the next week or so. By the third day, I began checking the main post office for a General Free Delivery envelope addressed to me, expecting my visa to arrive any day. I wasn't too concerned and it certainly was a nice break from the daily grind of traveling back and forth to the camp each day along dusty roads or working in the sweltering heat all day. Best of all, it was good to laugh, relax, and discover new things each day about Malaysia.

Two weeks had gone by and it was now May 13, 1981. It was Georgina's last day on the island.

We learned at breakfast that Pope John Paul II had been shot in St. Peter's Square in Vatican City. The tragedy was felt around the world. Later we would learn that, thankfully, he would survive. It was an almost tragedy that was felt around the world. It also made me realize that each day was a gift.

Saying good-bye to Georgina was harder than I anticipated, and I actually had to fight back the tears so she wouldn't wonder about me. We exchanged addresses at the ferry landing and promised to stay in touch. I decided to stop by the post office but once again was disappointed to see no visa had arrived yet. As I headed back to the hotel, I felt overcome with fear. What if the sisters had forgotten about me?

After bidding farewell to Georgina, I went back to my hotel room to lie down as I wasn't feeling very well. I had been a little light-headed and nauseated since waking that morning. As the afternoon went into evening, I started to worsen, and by the middle of the night, I was running a fever.

Sometime the next evening, there was a knock on the door but I was too weak to get up, so I said in a loud voice, "Who is it?"

Then a familiar Australian male voice came back, "Steve and the Banana Bender, which is slang for the Queenslander. The others are downstairs. Thought you might want to have a yarn since Georgina left and maybe get a bite?"

Trying to get up, I said, "Steve, that's really nice of you but I am not feeling well and really couldn't eat a thing. But I'll take a rain check, if that's okay?"

I could hear a little disappointment, "Ok, Yank. Hope you get to feeling better. Hooroo."

But when the knock came around ten the next morning, I was still in no shape to go anywhere, and apologized once again but what came back was, "Open the door, Yank. We're not leaving until you do. You can't stay here by yourself."

I shot back, "I'm in no shape to see anyone right now. I'm really sorry."

Steve insisted, "We don't care what you look like, we just want to make sure you're okay. Now please open the door."

It took all the strength I could muster to crawl out of bed and unlock the door. The look of concern on both Steve and Mac's faces scared me. They asked me a few questions and I told them I thought it was just another bad bout of amoebic dysentery and that it would probably clear up in a day or so. They insisted on taking me to a doctor. I told them I was extremely low on funds as I hadn't planned on being in Malaysia quite so long.

Steve said, "We thought that might be the case so we talked to our base commander, and he's given us permission to take you to Butterworth RAFB Hospital. So let's gather up your things and we'll get you looked after."

I couldn't believe they were going to such great lengths for someone they didn't even know, but I was truly grateful. I was pretty dehydrated, very weak, and very alone. The guys took me to the base hospital emergency room and once I was admitted, they promised to come by later. The hospital staff was friendly, and it was just my luck to get the best-looking doctor on base. He was at least six-foot-two, looked to be about thirty-five, with a full head of dark hair, piercing blue eyes, and an infectious smile. It was bad enough Steve and Mac had seen me at my worst, but this was worse because after running a number of tests and performing a very thorough examination, he performed a colonoscopy. I was later transported to the women's ward where a nurse promptly inserted a saline drip.

There were three other women sharing the ten-bed ward with me during my stay. They were equally as friendly, and all were married to airmen. They seemed to be enjoying their stay in Malaysia for the most part. Windows lined the two longest walls, and opened out to a covered veranda on either side of the ward. During the day, the shutter doors were opened to let the fresh air and light in, although there were screens on the windows to keep nature out.

After a brief chat with the ladies, I slept for what seemed like the longest time and woke up when I heard someone saying, "Hey, Yank!" I turned my head toward the sound of the voice and saw a group of guys led by Steve and Mac out on the veranda. The sight of these burly, rough and tumble soldiers outside my window with sheepish grins on their faces, all waving at "the Yank" made me laugh so hard it hurt. It really wasn't fair to invite them in since the other women were trying to recuperate, so I asked Steve to wheel me out on to the veranda for a bit.

Once they inquired as to how I was feeling, the usual banter began among the group. The guys, whose ages ranged from twenty-two to thirty-four, were full of jokes and stories about their lives on the base. They told about each other's escapades and it became obvious they were merciless with the endless pranks they pulled.

The visits became a daily routine for the five days that I was in the hospital. One of their favorite activities was to take turns reading silly, steamy romance novels to me which would guarantee fits of laughter all around.

Steve had agreed to check the mail for me, but there was still no word. When the doctor said I'd be discharged the next morning, the guys informed me that they had gotten permission to let me stay in the apartments on base until my visa was renewed. I couldn't believe it. Australian hospitality had no limits, and these homesick guys had literally saved my life.

They took me to a nicely furnished, two-bedroom apartment that belonged to the Red Cross for non-military guests on base. Although it was simple by Western standards, it felt luxurious to have a full kitchen with a sink, running water, a Western-style bathroom with a bath tub, soft towels, and a comfy bed. It even had a TV and a cassette player! A few of the guys brought me groceries for breakfast and lunch, and still others would take me to dinner with them every night. They even took me to the movies, which was a great treat since I hadn't seen an American movie in over a year.

By this time, it had been almost four weeks with no word from the sisters, and now when I saw Steve, I didn't ask about the mail anymore. When the weekend rolled around, the full gang came over with all the fixings for an Australian size cookout. They had steaks and chicken to put on the "barbie" along with coolers of beer, soda, and plenty of music. They were definitely in full relaxation mode. But somehow, I just wasn't feeling it. I tried to be polite, but it was obvious that I was not really up for having fun. Mac, who had been studying my face asked, "What's up, Yank? You don't seem all that cheerful today."

Steve chimed in, "Are the jokes getting old? Or are you feeling sick again? Have we over done it?"

Fighting back the emotion, I explained,

"I feel so ungrateful after all you've done for me but the truth is I'm worried. My tourist visa for Malaysia will expire in a week. I am flat broke and still have received no word from the sisters."

Steve stood up and reached into his back pocket, "This came about a week ago, but we thought you needed the rest before making the long trip back."

I opened the envelope and there was my visa, a train ticket, and some money to make the trip back to Ban Vinai. I didn't know whether to hug him or slug him but as I threw my arms up in the air, I shook my finger at him saying, "You stinker!"

When all the laughter died down, Mac and Steve pulled out a plaque with their battalion and squadron information on it along with the symbol of the Australian Royal Air Force and my name engraved on it.

"Yank," Mac handed the plaque to me, "In remembrance of our time together and in thanks for boosting our morale. Can't remember when we've laughed more since leaving home. It's been a pleasure and an honor. Now enough with the mushy stuff, I'm hungry. Break out the food!"

As the train made its way back to Bangkok, I transferred the addresses of all my new friends that I promised to keep in touch with, including Georgina and Vickie, into my permanent address book. I wrote a letter of thanks to the base commander to mail from Bangkok. It seemed so trivial compared to what they had done for me. Words can never express the respect and indebtedness I felt and still feel to this day.

Chapter 17

A month in Ban Vinai felt like six months back in the States. The days were long, the tropical heat was relentless, and the living conditions were crude at best, which is why most relief workers only stayed a few months at a time. I had experienced amoebic dysentery for many months and went down five dress sizes during my fifteen-month stay, which was a good thing. My body was tired of the crude living conditions, and after the Malaysian adventure it was time to move on. One of my Save the Children supervisors had shared information about a teaching opportunity in Mexico through the Experiment in International Living in Vermont. My plan was to learn Spanish so it would be easier to find a job in social services once I returned to the States. I had been offered a two month teaching position in Orizaba, Veracruz, Mexico at the Instituto Cultural Americano Norteamericano. I was to live with a Mexican family during my stay there in exchange for teaching full time at the institute.

Although I was sad to say good-bye to the sisters, my Thai friends in Chiang Khan, and my Ban Vinai friends, it was time for me to start making my way back to the United States, albeit via Mexico. There were two of us leaving the camp at the same time, and the going-away party included all the hospital staff from World Vision, the Red Cross, and COERR. While there was plenty of singing and reminiscing about our work during the time we had been together, I was truly touched when they gave me a Hmong quilt signed by everyone in the hospital.

Doctor Santos handed me a basket full of coins, saying "Carole, we wanted you to have this as a token of gratitude for all the babies whose lives were saved because of the respiratory therapy technique you introduced. The infant mortality rate has decreased by more than fifty percent since you began visiting the babies each day. Each coin represents all the babies whose lives you saved."

Chapter 18

The trip from Bangkok to Mexico City took thirty-six hours, with stops in Hong Kong, Taipei, Seoul, Tokyo, Los Angeles, and Dallas. There was an eight-hour layover in Los Angeles. This was my first look at the United States after traveling around Asia for more than a year. I realized just how much I had adapted to the conservative way of dress and behavior when I saw a blonde American girl on roller skates wearing Daisy Dukes, a skimpy halter top, headphones, with a cigarette hanging out of her mouth. I now understood the meaning of culture shock and realized why I was treated poorly in other countries from time to time.

As the plane touched down in Mexico City, I looked at the dirty, fraying strings that were hanging from both wrists and decided my journey from Bangkok to Mexico City was over so there was no need to keep them on any longer. The strings had been tied around my wrists by Hmong refugees at a farewell ceremony as part of a Buddhist blessing for "great luck, great riches, a great new job, and a safe journey." The practice of Sai Sin is especially popular in Northeast Thailand, where I had been living. I was told to wear the strings until they fell off, as to cut them off might bring bad luck.

While in Thailand, the strings seemed to have won me new found respect with the Thai people as I slowly made my way south toward Bangkok, taking one last look at the country where I had learned so much during the last fifteen months. Once I left Thailand, the strings elicited the same question of "What do the strings mean?" by every curious traveler I met en route from Bangkok to Mexico City. After two weeks, the once-white strings were now gray and more of a nuisance than a help. When the plane landed, I quickly cut them off and put them in my pocket.

The thirty-six-hour trip had taken its toll, but somehow as I made my way to the information counter at the airport, I felt a renewed sense of energy. I thought I could easily make the four-hour bus trip to Orizaba, Veracruz. When I reached the desk, the smiling hostess asked, "How may I help you, Miss?"

With every intention of completing my journey that day, I asked, "Can you please tell me how to get to the bus station to go to Orizaba?" Her response was totally unexpected,

"It's a four-hour ride to Orizaba, and you need to rest before traveling there. It is better for you to get a hotel today and after you rest, you can make the trip. Would you like me to arrange a hotel for you?"

Not giving up just yet, I said, "I'd rather get to the bus station, can you please help me do that?"

Unwavering, she said, "I'll help you get a hotel room so you can rest after your long trip. Then you can go to Orizaba in the morning."

As if it were settled, she made a call then pointed to the line of taxi's waiting outside the main exit, "Give this slip of paper to the driver."

Since I didn't speak Spanish, I could only hope the taxi driver spoke English. When I got to the first car in line, the driver quickly got out to help me with my luggage. "Do you speak English?" I asked.

He shook his head and replied, "No English."

I tried one last time to tell him the name of the bus station and town where I wanted to go, but he didn't understand so I handed him the slip of paper resigned to the fact that I would not be traveling to Orizaba that day, trusting that I would end up at a clean, safe, affordable hotel somewhere in Mexico City.

The ride to the hotel took about thirty minutes and as we weaved in and out of traffic through the streets of Mexico's historic capital, I couldn't help but compare it to Bangkok. There was a lot of traffic, smog and run-down areas in certain parts of town. As we neared the center of the city, the architecture became much more ornate, the streets were wider with beautiful plazas, fountains, and parks. There were street vendors at every light and political signs for the PAN and PRI parties plastered everywhere.

At long last, the taxi pulled up in front of a small, older hotel called the Hotel Valle. I paid the driver and made my way to the front desk with the luggage. Back then, my bags did not have wheels so I struggled with the bulging, oversized bag. The lobby was tiny but clean and obviously from a previous era, with its timeless worn marble and mahogany front desk, black and white tile floor, and brass fixtures. A silver-haired desk clerk with a moustache and glasses greeted me in English. I gave him the reservation slip from the airport courtesy desk, and he began to check me in asking me how long I intended to stay. I indicated I would only be staying for one night. When I pulled out my wallet, the clerk announced they only accepted credit cards or pesos. I indicated I only carried US dollars to which he offered, "I'll be glad to exchange your dollars for pesos, however the rate will be less favorable than a currency exchange place."

Under the circumstances, I had to accept whatever rate he was willing to pay since I had not thought to exchange my money at the airport. I gave him a hundred-dollar-bill in exchange for a handful of colorful bills that meant little to me at this point. Since I was paying cash, I had to settle in advance, and he promptly took several hundred pesos back. When I got to the room, I figured out the rate was higher than what I would normally agree to pay, but one night wouldn't hurt. I still had plenty left to get me to where I was going and to tide me over until I started teaching English.

The grumbling in my stomach reminded me that I hadn't eaten since I left Los Angeles eight hours ago, so I decided to grab something in the little coffee shop next to the lobby. Trying to decipher the menu was more of a challenge than what I anticipated, so I ordered *una hamberguesa con queso y tocino*, which I guessed to be a cheeseburger and something else. I figured if I didn't like whatever it was I would just put it to the side. It turned out to be a bacon cheeseburger with lettuce, tomato, and fries. Not too bad, I thought. Later I would learn it was the worst thing you could order in a Mexican restaurant.

After dinner, I decided to explore a bit while there was still daylight but realized I was pretty worn out and opted to return to the hotel. I laid down on the bed and the next thing I knew I was waking up with a violent urge to run to the bathroom. My head was spinning and the nausea was overwhelming. I washed my face, got into my pajamas and went back to bed only to repeat this same process over and over for the next forty-eight hours. I knew I had to get help and after several attempts to communicate with the front desk. The clerk kept hanging up on me. I found the number to the American Embassy in the phone book. Miracle of miracles, the clerk understood that I wanted to make a call, and fortunately I knew my numbers in Spanish. Much to my delight, the line was ringing and a male voice answered in American English, "United States Embassy," then went on to say, "We are currently closed in observance of Columbus Day and will re-open Tuesday, October 13." That was three days away. I would run out of money by then. I was so violently ill; at one point I just lay in the shower and turned the water on occasionally to rinse myself off.

After three days, I somehow got myself dressed, packed, and down to the front desk. It seemed like it took me forever. Once I paid the hotel, all I had left was $100. They had really taken advantage of me on the exchange rate, but I had little choice. I walked slowly to a taxi waiting at the curb. The driver helped with my luggage and stole occasional side glances at me as I gingerly made my way into the back seat of the taxi. My stomach and intestines were so distended and painful, I could not stand up straight nor could I sit normally. I had to lean as far back as possible so as not to bend my waist. Every move I made was excruciating. When I finally settled in to the cab, I glanced at the rear view mirror and saw the driver watching me.

I said, "ADO—Orizaba, por favor," which was the name of the terminal and the city I was going to. The driver glanced at me as he pulled away from the curb into traffic. As he darted in and out of the congested roadway, the pain from being jostled to and fro was more than I had ever experienced in my life. After a few minutes, the driver said, "You no go Orizaba."

I couldn't believe it. What was up with these people? First the woman in the airport refuses to help me get to Orizaba, now the taxi driver.

Once again I said, "Si, por favor, ADO a Orizaba."

He shook his head "No."

At which point, I closed my eyes and thought, I

guess this is it. It is the end of the road. I'm going to die in a foreign country and no one even knows I'm here.

After several turns, the driver turned and looked at me saying, "You no go Orizaba. You go doctor."

I laid my head against the back seat and closed my eyes. I could feel the tears streaming down my cheeks. I was too weak to protest any more. A few minutes later, the cab stopped in front of what appeared to be an elementary school. The driver got out, motioning me to wait and said, "Esperase."

He disappeared into the building and a few minutes later came out with a woman. They stood in front of the doors talking, looking at me from time to time. Then the woman disappeared inside the school and moments later reappeared only this time had another woman with her. All three of them approached the car and the second woman leaned forward as I rolled down the window.

In the most beautifully spoken English I had ever heard, she said, "My name is Mrs. Aleman, and this is Jose Hernandez and his wife, Maria del Carmen. Mr. Hernandez brought you here so that I could translate for him. He is concerned for your well-being and would like to take you to a doctor."

I began to recount the events of the last few days, trying to hold back the emotion, but it felt so good to finally be able to tell my story to someone who understood me. I explained that I had little money left and needed to use it to get to Orizaba.

"I have not been able to communicate with the director of the language institute to let her know I am in the country and explain why I did not arrive on time."

Mrs. Aleman kindly explained. "Mr. Hernandez will help you contact your director after taking you to see the doctor since there is no way you can make the trip in your current condition. Don't worry, they are good people, and you will be in good hands." Her smile reassured me and I was overcome with emotion.

"Thank you so much, Mrs. Aleman, and please thank Mr. and Mrs. Hernandez for me. I am so grateful for their kindness."

When she finished translating, Jose and his wife nodded and smiled at me. Jose drove me to a nearby clinic, and it was not long before I was ushered into an examining room where the doctor and Jose had to help me up on to the table, since I could hardly stand at this point. The pain in my lower intestines was unbearable.

The doctor introduced himself in perfect English. "I am Doctor Morales, and we are going to do this in stages, since you are in so much pain. First we will help you lay on your side, and then we'll help you roll over on to your back, okay?"

With tears streaming down my cheeks, I nodded, overcome once again with the joy of knowing that I was with someone I could communicate with and that I was about to get relief from the intense agony I had been experiencing for days. I answered questions about my general health and the incidents leading up to this point.

Then Doctor Morales said, "I am going to give you an injection that will alleviate the pain and antibiotics to eliminate the infection. Once I give you the shot, we will wait fifteen minutes for the medicine to take effect. Then I'll come back to check on you."

As I lay on the table waiting for the medication to take hold, I couldn't help but wonder what would have happened if I had not met Jose and his wife, Maria del Carmen. When the doctor returned, he asked, "Do you think you can sit up now?" Surprisingly, the pain was gone! In fact, I could even stand up straight.

"Whoa! Hold on, not so fast," Doctor Morales warned. "You are still in a very delicate state. You are extremely dehydrated, and if you don't continue with the shots every four hours, you will feel even worse than before. I'm going to give you a prescription, and Jose will take you to the pharmacy. You will then have to find someone to give you the injections for the next ten days. You must also stay on a clear liquid diet for the next few days. Please make plans to find a doctor in Orizaba who can do a follow-up exam to make sure you have healed properly."

I was so grateful and relieved at how much better I was feeling.

"Thank you so much, Doctor Morales. Where did you learn to speak such perfect English? Did you study in the States?" I wondered out loud.

He smiled and said, "Yes, I went to medical school at Loma Linda. I really had a hard time leaving but my family is here."

I smiled back and said, "I am very glad you did. Thank you again for coming to my rescue today. How much do I owe you?"

He graciously replied as he headed for the door, "You are very welcome, there is no charge for the visit and don't forget to follow up with a doctor in Orizaba."

After we picked up the prescriptions, we went to retrieve Jose's wife from school and they took me to their tiny three-room apartment, where they lived with their five children. The 400-unit apartment building was older and slightly run down. As we walked through the courtyard to the main entrance, the air was filled with the sounds and smells of families cooking, listening to music, children playing, dogs barking, and people arguing. As we climbed the four flights of stairs, I continued to marvel at how I could move about with ease. Jose insisted on lugging my suitcase upstairs, most likely because he feared for its safety if left in the taxi.

Jose's children greeted us at the door and the look of shock and surprise was clearly on their faces. The children, two boys and three girls, ranged in age from three to ten years old. Once inside the tiny apartment, Jose introduced me to the children who were wide-eyed and curious to know who this strange woman was that spoke no Spanish. While Jose and Maria del Carmen spoke to the children, I studied the small, over-crowded apartment and wondered how they could stand living such a cramped existence with no real privacy. It was evident, even without any understanding of the language, that this was a close-knit family and the children treated their parents with much respect. They motioned for me to sit on the day bed near the door, and when I sat down, the littlest one came and sat down next to me, staring at me the whole time.

Maria del Carmen offered a plate of food which I politely had to decline, motioning to my stomach, and she smiled knowingly. Jose then offered me a glass of lemonade, which I accepted to be polite but knew I could not drink. How could this family that had absolutely nothing be so generous and giving? Jose pointed to his watch, and then held an imaginary phone to his ear, indicating it was time for him to take me to call the director of the language institute in Orizaba. I so wanted to be able to help this family but did not have enough cash to make a difference, so I opened my suitcase and took out the most valuable item I had, the handmade king size Hmong quilt that had been given to me before I left Ban Vinai. I gave it to Jose trying to express my gratitude and explaining he could probably sell it for several hundred dollars. He and Maria del Carmen humbly and graciously accepted the quilt, thanking me for the gesture. I hugged them all and quickly left, as I felt close to tears and couldn't understand why.

True to his word, Jose took me to a public phone outlet and contacted the director of the language institute. She indicated to Jose that the best course of action was to take me to her brother's home in Mexico City, where I could spend the evening, and they would make sure I got to the bus station first thing in the morning. Jose handed me the phone and Gabriela Freeman, the executive director, explained.

"Carole, sounds like the best thing for you to do is get some rest, let the medication work a bit more before you travel, and we'll see you in a day or so." Then she gave me the address of the family in Orizaba where I was to go upon arrival.

In no time, Jose was pulling up in front of Mr. Freeman's home. After carrying my luggage to the front gate and ringing the door bell, Jose turned to shake my hand.

"Que le vaya con Dios," he said, "may you go with God."

Mr. Freeman came out to greet me, paid Jose, and helped me inside. I turned to watch Jose climb back into his run-down taxi. As he looked up and waved good-bye, I knew I would never forget his smiling face.

By this time the medication was beginning to wear off just as the doctor said it would, and I guess it was obvious as Mrs. Freeman gestured to the hallway.

"Welcome, Carole. The guest room is right this way if you would like to freshen up."

The room was tastefully decorated in an elegant French-style décor, almost picture perfect. It was in such contrast to Jose and Maria's tiny, cramped apartment. "I have called my neighbor, Raquel, who is a nurse. She will come by within the hour to inject your medicine."

A few minutes later, Mrs. Freeman returned with a cup of tea, which I later learned was chamomile. It was wonderful and just what I needed. As promised, Raquel came over to administer the medication and indicated she would come by in the morning. I decided to lie down just for a bit before joining the Freemans. I awoke to the sun pouring through the sheers that beautifully adorned the window. Outside, I could hear birds singing and the smell of coffee was wafting through the air. Once I showered and dressed, I made my way to the kitchen to apologize for being so rude. I found Mr. and Mrs. Freeman out on the covered patio filled with tropical plants. They were reading the paper and looked up and smiled as I came through the door.

"Buenos Dias, Carole. Did you sleep well? How are you feeling?"

They acted as if they had known me all my life and that it was no big deal that this perfect stranger had spent the night in their home.

"Do you think you could tolerate a cup of coffee?" It had been so long since I had eaten or drank anything beyond chamomile tea from the night before.

"Thank you so much. I'm not too sure about coffee but another cup of tea would be wonderful."

Smiling, Mrs. Freeman passed me a cup with a tea bag and the pitcher of hot water. "How about some toast?" as she passed me a spoon and the sugar bowl.

"I would love some toast!"

She turned towards the kitchen and asked, "Josefina, haga pan tostado para la senorita, por favor." In a few minutes, the maid brought in a plate of golden toasted bread.

"Raquel will be here in a little bit and once you are packed and ready to go, my husband will take you to the bus station, Carole. The medication is only good for about four hours, so it's best not to delay once Raquel leaves. My sister-in-law has made arrangements for a doctor to visit you when you arrive in Orizaba."

Wow, doctors in Mexico still made house calls? All the questions I seemed to have were being answered before I could ask them.

"Many thanks to both of you, I am forever grateful."

Mr. Freeman said good-bye after assisting me with the ticket purchase and checking my luggage. The ADO bus terminal was a huge circular building with a Plexiglas dome, which made it bright. The acoustics reverberated throughout the cavernous space every time the announcer came over the loud speaker. The station had doorways all around the circumference of the building with rows of people sitting and lines of people standing everywhere. This was a busy place with people traveling to all points south of Mexico City. It would be another thirty minutes before the bus to Orizaba was due to leave which gave me enough time to grow accustomed to the announcements and to learn to distinguish the names of the various destinations.

"Todos pasajeros a Puebla, favor de abordar el autobus numero seis cientos con salida a las diez y media," meant "All passengers going to Puebla, please board bus number 600 leaving at ten thirty." Above each door was a sign with the final destination written on it.

When I heard the announcer say, "Todos pasajeros a Orizaba…" I looked toward the door that said Orizaba and the people began to line up and so I did too. I made my way onto the bus and by the time it was ready to leave, every seat was filled. As the bus made its way out of the city towards the highway, I began to settle in with a book for the four-hour trip. I felt unusually tired, and it was barely noon, so I closed my eyes for a bit and when I opened them, the bus was bouncing in and out of pot holes as it made its way into the parking lot of the bus station in Orizaba. As I sat up, the bus hit a huge pot hole and jostled me so hard that I lost a contact lens. The windows were tinted and it was hard to see where it had fallen. I searched long after everyone had disembarked but couldn't find it anywhere.

I got off the bus and went to retrieve my luggage and saw the luggage doors were closed. The driver pointed to the station so I went inside the terminal and saw two people behind the luggage counter. I handed them my ticket and when they slid my suitcase toward me, I placed the cassette player I was carrying on the ground next to my feet. I leaned over to get the suitcase and struggled in my weakened state. When I finally got it down off the counter and onto the floor, I turned to pick up the cassette player, and it was gone.

I looked at the row of passengers that were seated facing me, and expressionless faces stared back. "Did you see a radio?" I pointed to the floor and outlined the shape of the cassette player but the faces continued to stare blankly back at me. I turned

144

to the people behind the luggage counter and repeated the same question and gestures, but they shrugged their shoulders, shook their heads, and lifted their palms in the universal gesture of "I don't know."

A taxi driver who spoke a little English approached me, "You need help?" Gratefully, I explained what had happened, and he asked the people sitting there if they saw anything.

"They saw nothing, Miss. You need a taxi?" I pulled out the piece of paper with the contact information of the family where I was supposed to stay and gave it to the driver, as he looked at the address, picked up my suitcase and said, "This way, please." We drove for about ten minutes and he pulled up in front of a vacant lot. "This is the place."

Somehow I had the wrong address. "Do you know Gabriela Freeman?" How many Mexican nationals in a town the size of Orizaba would have a German surname? The driver shook his head.

Fortunately, I remembered that I had the address of the family my supervisor in Thailand had lived with, the Gonzalez family. I showed the driver the address and within a few minutes we were in front of the Gonzalez home. It was dark now as I climbed out of the taxi. The driver placed my suitcase on the sidewalk saying, "That will be 150 pesos." In 1981, that was the equivalent of $12.50 for a ride that should have cost no more than $2.50. As I started to protest, the front door to the home opened and out came a good-looking young man, "May I help you?" he said in perfect English.

I introduced myself and explained all that had transpired since arriving in Orizaba ending with, "And now this man wants to overcharge me for a fifteen-minute ride from the bus station."

The young man spoke quickly to the driver, then paid him the 150 pesos much to my dismay saying,

"It's better if we just let this one go. I am Gerardo Gonzalez, would you like to come in?"

As the taxi drove away, I peered through the beautiful wrought iron archway into the exquisite marble foyer of the Gonzalez home and followed Gerardo into the stately residence.

Once inside, two older women came from the kitchen into the foyer, one approached us and started asking Gerardo questions in Spanish. While Gerardo explained the situation, the woman, whom I would later learn was his mother, kept glancing at me from time to time with a kind expression on her face. The other woman stayed in the background just listening. Later I would learn it was Teresita, the maid.

Gerardo turned to me and said, "Carole, this is my mother, Gloria Gonzalez."

"Mucho gusto, Carolina," to which I replied, "Mucho gusto."

Gerardo explained, "My Mother will call Gabriela Freeman to get the correct address of the family you are to stay with and then I will take you there. Why don't you come and sit in the living room? Can I get you anything?"

Looking around, I said, "May I use your bathroom?"

To which he replied, "Of course, right this way."

By now the medication was really starting to wear off, and I was once again reminded that I was still in delicate shape. When I came out of the bathroom, I could hear everyone talking in the kitchen. I took a seat on the sofa waiting for them to come back. The house smelled wonderful, making it obvious that I had interrupted dinner preparation. Gerardo came back into the room with his mother, who came and sat next to me on the sofa.

"How are you feeling? Gabriela told us of your food poisoning." As Gerardo spoke, Mrs. Gonzalez took my hand and squeezed it.

"The medication is wearing off and it's been a long day." I said wearily.

Mrs. Gonzalez looked at me, "Quieres una taza de te? Te?" She gestured like she was sipping tea.

"Si, por favor," I answered, gratefully accepting her offer.

As she left the room, she said something to Gerardo and he looked at me. "My mother says you need to stay here. Gabriela told her you have medication that needs to be injected?"

I nodded to which he said, "My mother will get someone to give it to you. In the mean time, I will show you to the guest room." He picked up my bag and headed up the stairs as if all was settled, so I followed, not wishing to turn down a place to rest.

"You go ahead and settle in. If you need anything, just call me. Our home is your home."

Humbled by the genuine hospitality, I could feel my eyes well up as I said, "Thank you so much."

Once I settled in under the covers, Mrs. Gonzalez was knocking on the door with the tea and their neighbor from across the street was with her. Gerardo explained that she was going to administer the medication since she used to be a nurse before she got married, and then he left. All I could do was smile and repeatedly say, "Gracias."
I woke up around two a.m. and Mrs. Gonzalez was at my side, giving me the antibiotics, putting a cool cloth on my head and taking my temperature.

This went on for several days with trips to the bathroom being the only reason I got out of bed. I was in excruciating pain when the medication wore off. The pain had extended to my joints and every muscle in my body. The doctor came twice during the week to examine me. He diagnosed a severe case of trichinosis caused from the bacon-burger I had eaten at the hotel. Recovery would be slow and it would be a few weeks before I could even start teaching. Throughout the whole process, Mrs. Gonzalez took care of me day and night. She was so sweet and so loving that the tears rolled down my cheeks one night as she hovered over me in the middle of the night, washing me with a cool cloth, giving me warm broth, antibiotics, and staying with me until I went back to sleep.

Chapter 19

The recovery process was slow but after two weeks I was able to start teaching one class a day. By the end of the first two months, I was teaching three classes in the morning and five classes in the evening from four to nine p.m. In the early 1980s, Orizaba was a small city with a population of about 250,000 inhabitants. The streets were named north, south, east and west and the inner city streets were named numerically with Colon Oriente and Francisco Madero Street being dividing lines. This made getting around on my own easy. However the Gonzalez family insisted that someone accompany me at all times. It wasn't acceptable for me to be alone on the street, so the family and my students took turns walking me to and from school each day, twice a day.

Orizaba is located at the base of the snow-capped Pico de Orizaba, an inactive volcano and the highest mountain in Mexico, the third highest in North America. The climate was fairly moderate with temperatures in the low sixties in January, mid- nineties in July, and a higher-than-average rainfall of about sixty inches per year. This made for lush vegetation in Orizaba and surrounding areas like Fortin de las Flores and Cordoba that were famous for their beautiful flowers and aromatic coffee.

Since English was taught in elementary and secondary schools, the majority of my students were adults. The morning classes were made up of professionals and their wives wishing to learn English for business or travel purposes. The afternoon classes were predominantly filled with college students and working adults. Occasionally, I had classes with younger students whose parents wanted them to learn English from a native speaker. I received room and board from the family in exchange for teaching their children English, and I received a small stipend of 3000 to 4000 pesos a month for eight classes a day, five days a week. Initially, this was equivalent to about $250 to $330 a month. My goal was to stay long enough to become fluent in Spanish, which I thought would take no more than six months. That would give me sufficient time to save up enough money for a ticket home with a little bit left over to live on for a few months until I found a job.

Life with the Gonzalez family was wonderful. They were a warm and gracious family with four boys who ranged in age from ten to twenty-six years old and one daughter, Gloriacita , who was fourteen and very smart. Gloriacita and Gerardo were the only members of the family who spoke English. The two oldest young men worked with Mr. Gonzalez in his cement business while Gerardo was away at college during the week. Gloriacita and her younger brother were in school during the day and busy with after-school activities. This really forced me to learn to communicate on my own since Mrs. Gonzalez and Teresita, the maid, spoke no English at all. Of course, the first words I learned revolved around meal times and food. Once I had recovered, the best part of each day was trying something totally new at each meal. All I can say is that ignorance is bliss when it comes to trying new things because in some cases, had I really known what I was about to eat, I never would have experienced the savory, delightful experience of true Southern Mexican cuisine.

My absolute favorite time of the day was mid-morning between classes when Mrs. Gonzalez and Teresita would make appetizers called *picaditas* and *memelitas* with refried black beans. They are made by hand just like corn tortillas, but picaditas, meaning "little pinched ones," are pinched around the edge to form a ridge to keep in the salsa, diced onions, and cheese that are added after the maza is toasted on the comal. Memelitas are made just like tortillas but when the maza is rolled into a ball, refried beans are inserted into the maza ball, sealed, flattened, and cooked on the comal. Once cooked, they are topped with salsa, onions, whey, or cheese. These were served with fresh café, made just like the cowboys made it on the open range in a tin coffee pot over an open flame.

The Gonzalez family graciously remained my host family for the first two months, and I had really begun to get attached to them when Gabriela, or "Gabi" as everyone called her, told me that it was time to stay with another family. It was customary for a family to host for no more than eight weeks. So it was with great reluctance and sadness that I moved to another host home. This time it was Gabi's secretary and her family who generously opened their modest home to me. While they were kind, the house was tiny, and it was obvious someone had given up their room for me. After a month or so, I began to look for a room to rent.

In addition to having to pay for my own room and board, another major event occurred that further delayed my return to the United States. I was in class one day and one of my students, an engineer, asked me what I thought about the devaluation that had occurred earlier that morning. Having no idea what that meant, he went on to explain, "The economy is so poor in Mexico that the peso has lost much value against the U.S. dollar. So instead of twelve pesos for every one U.S. dollar, it now costs twenty-four pesos to buy one U.S. dollar." Being young and naïve, I thought surely this doesn't apply to me? Reality set in when I went to the bank to pull out the four hundred U.S. dollars I had deposited over the last several months. I got back less than two hundred after the bank deducted its fees.

On the bright side, teaching in Mexico was so much fun as teachers are highly respected. For the most part, English-language students attend a private institute because they want to learn. The courses were eight weeks long and there were nine levels. Most of my students were at the intermediate to advanced level since the classes were taught entirely in English. I had now been teaching for almost six months and my Spanish was improving along with my teaching skills.

One day as the first class of students began to enter my classroom, they greeted me with "Felicidades, Maestra," which confused me because it wasn't my birthday, and it wasn't a holiday so I just smiled and said

"Gracias!"

I figured it would soon be revealed as is everything when you are not familiar with a culture or the customs. Then a few more students entered, greeting me in the same way, bearing colorfully wrapped gifts. Now I knew that they surely were under the impression that it was my birthday. I wondered who could have told them that, but as sweet as it was, I needed to set the record straight so I politely explained that I could not accept the gifts because it was not my birthday. They all smiled as one student explained, "Es el Dia de su Santo," while another translated, "It's St. Caroline's Day. Felicidades!" Amazingly, I was showered with greetings and gifts for the entire day. What an amazing place.

A week or so later, the same routine began all over again and this time I immediately addressed the situation, smiling at my students sheepishly. "I thank you, once again, for your kindness but I am sure it is not my saint's day or my birthday so I am embarrassed to say I do not understand why we are celebrating."

With this, they all chuckled politely and said, "Es el Dia de la Maestra. Felicidades, Maestra!" "It's Teacher's Day. Congratulations, Teacher!"

And once again, I was treated like a queen all day long with a party in each class, lots of gifts, hugs, and well wishes. I was truly touched by the generosity and goodwill I continued to experience in this wonderful colonial place from days gone by.

While most of the families I met were not extremely well to do, life in Orizaba was rich with good food, friends, and time with family. One of my best friends was a former student from the institute, an industrial engineer named Gustavo, who had recently returned from a summer spent in the United States on an exchange program. We met at the institute because Gabi had invited him to share his travel experiences with the students enrolled in the advanced classes. Gabi asked Gustavo to walk me home that first night and it was nice to be able to speak English with someone my age who understood everything I was saying. While Gabi was fluent, she was in her sixties and insisted I speak to her in my haltingly limited Spanish.

Gustavo must have enjoyed practicing his English because every night after my last class, I would find him waiting for me with the offer to walk me home. We would stop for a light supper on the way, sometimes talking late into the night. Then he'd safely escort me back to the Gonzalez home. Our favorite thing to do on weekends was travel to Cordoba, Veracruz which was only thirty minutes away where we would enjoy the folk dancers on the church plaza and sit across the street on the terrace of Los Portales de Cordoba. We would begin by drinking *un lechero* served in a tall fountain glass. There were waiters who came by and poured the dark coffee first, and then we'd tap our glasses with a spoon to let another waiter know we were ready for the hot milk to be poured. The milk was followed by a little sprinkle of cinnamon and a basket of sweet bread. We would sit and lazily read the paper and visit with friends as they would come and go all day long. After coffee and sweet bread, we'd have brunch, visit some more, watch the folk dancers across the street on the plaza in front of the cathedral, and then we'd head home for an afternoon siesta.

After a few years of working for Gabi for about one hundred fifty U.S. dollars per month, Gustavo asked me to marry him and I accepted. Gustavo was an intelligent and kind man who was very close to his family. We had high hopes of starting a family of our own once Gustavo advanced a little further in his career. Just before the wedding, I decided to take a little time off. I had been teaching full time, year round, for two solid years. After the honeymoon, I planned to move on to other more lucrative opportunities so that I could eventually go home. I had earned a solid and respected reputation in the community and was offered a teaching job at the local university that I was seriously considering.

One day, the doorbell rang and it was one of my former students wanting to know if I would consider giving her private lessons. I told her I would think about it and would get back with her. Then another student called that week asking if I would teach him and his friend, also a former student. By the second week, I had twelve students and was earning more in one week than I had in a month when I taught for Gabi. It eventually evolved into a private school, and I recruited recent college grads from the United States to come and help me teach. I truly enjoyed teaching and my students became an extended family for me. I learned so much more from them than they did from me.

From time to time, I would hear that Gabi was extremely unhappy with me because I became the competition. Verbal threats would come my way via mutual friends, and it was always upsetting. Gabi's discontent with me became well known. This went on for years until the day before I left Orizaba. It was teacher's day, and I stopped by the market to purchase a bouquet of flowers. I went to Gabi's house, rang the bell, and when she opened the door, she could not hide the look of surprise.

I handed her the flowers, "Gabi, please accept these as a token of my deep appreciation for bringing me to Orizaba and for all that you have done for me."

She opened the door wider as she accepted the peace offering. "Would you like to come in for a cup of coffee?"

We chatted a bit over coffee, mostly small talk and then I handed her a card, "Once again, thank you for everything. Here's my address in Ciudad Juarez and please know that my house is always your house."

Several months later, a former American teacher who had taught in Orizaba called from New

York. I was surprised to hear her voice. "How did you find me?" I asked.

With a sense of surprise in her voice, she said, "I recently visited Orizaba and ran into Gabi. She had nothing but good things to say about you and offered your contact info. What did you do to make that happen?"

Chapter 20

Leaving my students and friends in Orizaba was so difficult but Gustavo had been given a scholarship to study his master's in Industrial Engineering in Ciudad Juarez, Chihuahua while still receiving a full salary. It was a great opportunity, and it was on the border with El Paso, Texas. This would give me a chance to look for work in the United States again. We both agreed the political instability and the growing drug trade in Mexico was a reason to think about eventually moving back to the United States.

The first six months in Juarez were difficult at best. Even though at the time it was considered one of the better border cities, it still left a lot to be desired. It lacked the traditional pomp and circumstance of the interior towns and cities I had come to know and love about Mexico. Being a border city, Juarez was more dependent on the American economy for economic survival. The twin-plant industry had created a population explosion as workers from all over Mexico moved to the border in search of higher wages and steady work in the manufacturing industry. The city infrastructure could not keep pace with the demand for water, sewer, and utilities. As housing became scarce, those who could not afford to build were forced to live in cardboard and cinder block colonias on the outskirts of the city with no utilities. It was dirty, dusty, and the crime rate was growing steadily. There was a great deal of fear toward law enforcement since it was ripe with corruption.

The U.S. economy had slowed considerably and unemployment along the border was extremely high. Without connections, it took me more than a year and a half to land a part time job at Wal-Mart. A few months later, we sold our house in Juarez and found an apartment in El Paso. After living outside the United States for almost seven years, I was finally going home. I pulled along side the truck with all our belongings that was parked in the customs inspection area on the U.S. side of the border. Not knowing what to expect, I had carefully numbered all the boxes and made a detailed list of what was contained in each box. I was prepared to spend hours if they felt it necessary to examine each box.

The customs agent asked for my passport and after reviewing it carefully, looked at me then looked at the cargo truck lined with boxes and furniture. Noticing the numbers, he said in a very serious tone, "What's in box number twenty-four?"

I looked down my list and smiling politely, I offered, "Books."

He reached for the box, opened it and saw it was crammed with books in all shapes and sizes. "What's in box number eight-nine?"

Once again, I ran my finger down the list and said, "Housewares."

When he opened the box filled with housewares, he looked up at me and smiled, "You've been away for a long time. Welcome home, young lady." He closed the box, then closed the truck's doors, tipped the brim of his hat towards me and waived the truck on through. Although I had driven across the border hundreds of times during the last two years, this time it felt different, this time I was home.

Chapter 21

The five-year marriage had been rocky from the start with Gustavo returning home to live with his mother right after we returned from the honeymoon. His mother was having a hard time adjusting to the fact that her son was no longer living with her, which manifested itself in various mysterious health problems. The problems miraculously cleared up when Gustavo moved back home. After a few weeks, Gustavo finally returned with no money. He had given it all to his family even though we really needed it. It was summer break at the technological institute where Gustavo taught engineering classes. There would be no paycheck for another six weeks. Throughout our tumultuous marriage, this was a reoccurring theme.

Now in 1988, I was four months pregnant with my first child, and it was my birthday. I had the day off from Wal-Mart, where I worked as a claims clerk. I slept in a bit then got up after Gustavo left for work. After five years of marriage, we were finally going to have a baby. We had tried to have children for the last three years and had all but given up.

I opened the laundry hamper and the smell of cigarette smoke hit me in the face. The clothes

Gustavo had worn the day before were on top. He had come in after midnight so no doubt he had gone to a bar with the guys after work. Gustavo was an industrial engineer and worked in the automotive twin plants in Ciudad Juarez, just on the other side of the border. I began to pull the clothes out and something on his shirt caught my eye. It was so cliché, I had to smell the red smudge on his collar to convince myself of what my eyes were seeing. The collar and shoulder smelled of stale, cheap perfume. Just like that, my world was upside down. Gustavo moved out a week later.

When I got so swollen that I couldn't get my shoes on, I realized I was going to have to stop working. But then what? I remember crying over the phone to my best friend, Lucinda.

"I just don't know how to keep it all going when I have no control over my life right now. Each day, my wardrobe gets smaller and I can barely fit behind the wheel of the car!"

After we laughed through my tears, she said, "Carole, you're just going to have to swallow your pride and tell your husband he has to move back in to support you until you can support yourself and the baby."

I remember thinking there's not chance in this world that I would lower myself to that level after I discovered that he had been seeing other women five months earlier.

Through all the uncertainty, Lucinda Rice was my rock. Her support and caring ways were critical during the emotional roller coaster I found myself on. As if reading my thoughts, my friend Lucinda went on to say,

"You have to think about the baby now and forget about how you feel."

It hit me like a ton of bricks. It was no longer just about me, I had a life growing inside me that I was now responsible for and had no way to support myself, let alone a child. She was right, I thought as I fought back a wave of nausea.

My husband saw me through the delivery of our ten-pound fifteen-ounce baby boy, Vincent, who was born four days early, on December 21, 1988. As I gazed at the perfect little baby boy in my arms, it was hard to believe that I could ever love him more than I did in that moment. The amazing thing was that with each passing day, my love for him grew greater. By the time Vincent was a month old, it became even more difficult to fathom how my own parents could be so uninvolved in my life. But none of that mattered because now that he was here it was time to put a plan together. I had been blessed with a healthy child and would soon be able to go back to work.

When my husband had initially moved out, I sold my new car for what I owed to get rid of the monthly payments and bought an eleven-year-old clunker that ran fine the day I test drove it. A few weeks later, it turned out to have electrical problems. The various trips to the mechanic had really eaten up the tiny amount I had in the checking account prior to the baby being born. I was so desperate, I even filled out an application for food stamps and welfare benefits. I had second thoughts when I drove to the parking lot of the local food stamp office and could not muster the courage to go inside. I chose to go without, tore up the application and turned the car around to head back home determined to find a better way.

Four weeks after my son was born, my boss at Wal-Mart called and wanted to know when I was coming back to work. I told him the doctor would release me in four more weeks since it was a Caesarian delivery. Two weeks later, he called again to say he really needed me to come back to work. I told him I was breast feeding and still did not have a doctor's release.

He replied, "Stick a bottle in his mouth and get back to work."

I refused and hung up, knowing that I had just burned a bridge. But I couldn't support the baby on that salary anyway. It was so stressful to watch the few remaining resources I had dwindle each day while I applied for jobs and desperately waited for the phone to ring. My son was twelve weeks old, my marriage had fallen apart, and I hadn't received a paycheck in three and a half months. There was nothing left in the bank account and we were now living off of my credit card. There was enough of a balance to keep us going for another month's rent, diapers, baby food, and gas if I only used the car to run to the store and for job interviews.

I had applied for so many different positions. The problem was trying to find a job that had benefits and paid enough to cover our living expenses, which would include daycare. The one job I truly hoped I would hear back from was with the Texas Department of Human Services as a case worker in the income assistance program. The entry level salary was $17, 500 a year to start, and the benefits were good. I had taken the exam and scored fairly high. I know it seems ironic that I was willing to help others with the same benefits I refused to accept for myself and my son. During my early years with my mother, we were dependent on public assistance and I did not want to follow in her footsteps. The last time I called to check on the status of filling the positions, I was told there was a hiring freeze in place with no estimated end date.

With no prospects on the horizon, I had just enough money to get me through one more month and to rent a U-Haul truck. I notified the landlord on the first of the month and made plans to head back to Massachusetts in hopes of finding a job there. I remember getting down on my knees in front of my son's crib and offering up a prayer that if given the opportunity to serve others, I would never forget what this moment felt like. All I needed was enough to support my baby and keep a roof over our heads. By mid-month, I had packed up most of our belongings leaving only what we needed for the next few weeks. Then the call I had been waiting for came. The hiring freeze was going to be lifted by the first of the month and my name was at the top of the list.

Chapter 22

The hardest question I ever had to answer was posed by my four-year-old son, Vincent. We were playing with matchbox cars on the living room floor and out of the blue he asked, "Mommy, who is my grandpa on your side of the family?"

I don't know why I had never anticipated my son asking this question. I guess I just put all the painful memories on the shelf and went about trying to build a better life for myself.

That night, after I tucked my son into bed, I began to think about his question and all the ramifications behind it. The last time I had tried reconnecting with my dad was when I was in the hospital in Boston. It was clear that he truly had washed his hands of me as he warned me he would when I told him I wanted to move out of his parents' home to attend college.

So after all these years, why would I want to call him? Why should I put myself out there and be rejected all over again? I tossed and turned all night with all the painful memories coming back to the forefront of my mind. All these years, I had always felt a deep ache, a huge emptiness inside. It was hard to be alone, especially with a child. But it had made me stronger. I was a survivor. When I woke up the next day and saw my little boy's beautiful smile, I realized that it was no longer about me. So with great trepidation, I picked up the phone and dialed the number that I hadn't dialed in eighteen years but that I still knew by heart. It was a wonder I could hear it ringing over the sound of my heartbeat, which seemed deafening. I decided I would hang up if no one answered after the fourth ring and then I heard a woman's voice with that familiar New England accent say, "Hulloh."

"Mary, is that you?"

She answered, "Yes," in typical New England cadence that turned a one syllable word into two.

I continued, "It's been a long time since we've spoken so you probably don't recognize my voice."

She said, "I know it sounds familiar, but I just can't place it yet."

Ending the mystery, "It's me, Carole."

With an obvious tone of shock in her voice she said, "I never thought this day would come."

I told her where we were living and then told her I was divorced and had a son who was asking about his grandfather. "Would Dad be open to meeting him?" I ventured.

"I'll have to talk to him and let you know."

I gave her my phone number and hung up. About a week later, we came home to find a message on the recorder that said, "Carole, this is your father. Just calling to see how you are. Call me when you get a chance." And there it was; the door was open once again.

Within a few months, we had exchanged photos and made plans to spend ten days together. I had also reconnected with my dad's parents and sister. Slowly but surely we found our way back. My most meaningful memory is that of reconnecting with my paternal grandfather the day after he had heart surgery.

When he heard my voice for the first time in more than twenty two years, he exclaimed,

"Oh, Carole, I always loved you."

Unfortunately Grandma Marie was experiencing severe memory loss and often did not know who I was. My Aunt Elaine has become a source of strength and support over the last eighteen years, and I am grateful for her presence in my life. While nothing can replace the lost years, the anger and hurt have given way to understanding and forgiveness.

Chapter 23

Our life in El Paso was comfortable. I had a steady job as an assistant supervisor in the Income Assistance Department for the Texas Department of Human Services. I had the best boss anyone could wish for. Ofelia Melendez was so supportive and appreciative of my work and of me. She never missed an opportunity to champion my cause. I loved our little house that was located on a quiet cul de sac with the best neighbors. We watched each other's children, helped each other with home repairs and yard work, and formed a Neighborhood Watch program to help keep the area safe. It was a very comfortable life, in fact so comfortable, it felt complacent.

The silent nagging to move forward with my life turned into a full-blown effort on my part to get a promotion, even if it meant moving to another city. Although I kept wrestling with the whole idea because my life was so comfortable, inherently I knew if I was going to grow and provide more opportunities for Vincent, El Paso was not going to be that place.

In December 1994, I accepted a supervisory position in Houston and the day after Christmas, we packed up all our earthly possessions into a twenty-six-foot U-Haul, towing the car on the back end. We made the drive to our new home in Katy, Texas in just under seventeen hours. The adjustment was bumpy at first but it was for the best. A year later, I became engaged to my current husband, Keith. We were married in 1996 and in May 1997 we welcomed our daughter Victoria into our lives to complete our family.

Chapter 24

I was sitting in my Houston office not long after I had accepted a position to oversee a faith-based community ministry in 1998. I stared at a plaque on the wall that read, "As for me and my house, we shall serve the Lord, Joshua 24:15." The realization came to me that the sum of all my experiences became my life's work.

That morning, I had arrived at the ministry to find a homeless woman sitting on a dingy, stained, donated sofa that had been placed at the back door. She was reading a novel while she gingerly took a puff on her cigarette. When she saw me pull up, she put her book down and flicked her cigarette out into the parking lot.

"Good morning." I said as I approached the door. "How are you doing today?" I said smiling at her.

"I've been better," she candidly replied with a hint of a smile forming at the corners of her mouth.

The warm Houston sun was already beaming down on us as I looked at the sofa blocking the doorway and asked,

"Would you mind giving me a hand so I can unlock the door?"

"You bet!" she said eagerly.

"People are generous with their donations but for some reason they don't see the drop off area around the side of the building." I explained.

As the woman helped me unblock the doorway so that I could unlock the door, she told me her story. Her car broke down and she could not afford the repair. Without the car, she could not get to work, so she lost her job. She was currently sleeping on a friend's couch, the third living situation since she lost her apartment. The hardest part about moving around so much is that when she applies for jobs and employers call back, she does not get the messages until it's too late.

"If I had a phone number with a voice mail box that I could check whenever I can access a phone, I would appear more stable to potential employers, and I could call them back before they hire someone else."

Perhaps we could look into putting in a dedicated line and expanding the voice-mail system to provide this service, I thought. I made a mental note to look into it.

"For now, I just need some help getting my car repaired and perhaps a little money for gas so I can keep looking for a job."

I told her to make herself comfortable in the waiting area and explained the ministry wouldn't be open for a few hours. It was still some time before seven a.m., and the volunteers typically started interviewing at ten. She said she had heard it was on a first come, first served basis, which is why she had arrived at dawn.

I showed her where the bathrooms were and asked, "Have you had anything to eat today?"

She shook her head no and quickly said, "I'm not much of a breakfast person but I am a little hungry."

I smiled understandingly, "Okay, have a seat and I'll be back in a bit."

As I walked into the food pantry that was abundantly filled with canned goods, meat, cheese, frozen foods, and donations of bread and pastries from local grocers and bakeries, I felt blessed to be able to give her something to tide her over until the volunteers arrived.

She looked embarrassed but grateful as I handed her some juice and breakfast rolls and said,

"Thanks, I appreciate it."

I answered, "My name is Carole," as I extended my hand towards her, she quickly shifted the food to free her right hand as she eagerly shook mine.

"I'm Alice."

"It's nice to meet you Alice," picking up the bag and heading to my office. "I'm going to try and get some work done before the rest of world gets here. Staff and volunteers will be arriving shortly and they'll get you signed in. I appreciate your patience and I hope things get better for you soon. Take care and thanks for the idea about the voice mail."

As I walked to my office, I couldn't help but think about what Alice was going through and how humiliating and unsettling it was to have to live off of friends and move around every few days. I wondered what had led her to this point in her life. She appeared healthy and showed no signs of drug or alcohol abuse. Although she looked tired and disheveled, she seemed otherwise capable of becoming independent again.

I put my bag down under my desk after removing my Day-Timer with my to-do list. I quickly jotted down "voice mail" so I wouldn't forget and then looked at the items on the page to see what I could knock out quickly before the phones started ringing and the lines began to form. By ten o'clock, the ministry was in full swing, the lobby was full, and as I passed through to check on how many volunteers had arrived, the receptionist was calling Alice's name. She smiled as I said, "Things are bound to get better, just hang in there."

She looked at me gratefully, her eyes filling a bit as she said, "They can't get any worse." As I went through the assistance program doors, I shuddered to think what was behind her words and said a silent prayer for her and all the Alices in this world.

As I went back in to my office, both lines were ringing, I put one on hold and answered the other, "This is Carole, how may I help you?" The voice on the other end responded, "Hello, I'm Margaret Donovan with Houston Community Voice Mail. We provide free voice mail for homeless individuals to assist them on their journey to independence. We do this by partnering with other nonprofit organizations. This is a free service that we would like to provide through your ministry. It will not cost the ministry anything to participate. Is this something you might be interested in?"

After five months of serving at the ministry, it was evident that there was a reason for all that happened and a purpose to everything. This was and still is the greatest lesson I have learned.

It was the day before Christmas and although the ministry was closed, I decided to go in to the office for a few hours to finish the paperwork that had been piling up so I could truly enjoy my time off with family. The last several days had been filled with so much hustle and bustle as volunteers worked tirelessly to distribute gifts and food to hundreds of families in need. Miraculously, we seemed to have enough to serve not only those who had pre-registered but those families who came at the last minute in hopes of finding something to put under the tree.

The months and weeks leading up to Christmas distribution required attending nighttime and weekend events held by local groups and businesses that partnered with us to raise the needed donations. Since I had a relatively small staff at the time, in addition to overseeing the daily operations, I was the only fund raiser, which left little time to tend to home and family. As I drove to the ministry, thinking about the long list of tasks I needed to complete for my own family to enjoy the holidays, I couldn't understand why I felt compelled to go in to the office.

As I pulled in to the parking lot, I noticed a fairly new car was parked by the back door near the food pantry. Our ministry was blessed with so many donations from individuals and local businesses in the community that we were able to leave a basket of free baked goods and bread in a vestibule for anyone in the community to access anytime. A well-dressed man who appeared to be in his late sixties or early seventies was carrying baked goods and walking toward his car. He looked at me sheepishly as I greeted him.

"Good morning," while simultaneously putting my hand in my purse to pull out the key to the building.

"You're probably wondering why I came here to get free bread," said the man.

The thought had crossed my mind and I had struggled to keep it from showing on my face but had obviously failed.

"It's okay, no need to explain," I turned to look at him and smiled, ashamed of myself for making him feel so uncomfortable. "The bread is there for anyone to access so feel free to help yourself."

He seemed to ignore my feeble attempt to put him at ease saying,

"Up until recently, I was driving a car that was fourteen years old. It kept breaking down so often, my son was concerned that I might get stranded. He's an engineer and has done well for himself."

I smiled politely, "Oh, how nice!"

"Yes, it was hard for me to accept his help because I once worked for Shell Oil and had a very high-paying position. It enabled me to buy a nice home, put my kids through college, and save enough to retire early, or so I thought."

I held the door open for him and we entered the lobby of the ministry to get out of the cold. "You really don't need to explain, it's okay. We are here for the entire community and the bread is there for all to take." I really felt terrible.

He went on, ignoring me once again, "Then my wife was diagnosed with cancer and the medical bills ate up all our savings and continued to pile up. Even with my pension and social security, we barely seem to scrape by because her medication is so expensive. Since we are eligible for Medicare, we do not qualify for coverage under Shell's medical benefits anymore. While it's a small thing, the free bread and pastries help "

Heading toward the food pantry, I asked, "Have you applied for our senior food program? By the way, I'm Carole Little," I extended my hand toward him.

"Richard Hanson." His hand shake was warm and strong. "Yes, I actually met with someone several months ago but they said with my pension and our social security, we don't qualify."

I made a mental note to look for his file. "Before you leave, please be sure to leave me your contact information. I'd like to look into a few things for you, if that's okay?"

He nodded gratefully, tears filling his eyes. I turned away quickly, busying myself with getting a bag and loading it up with fruits and vegetables. "Do you have plans for Christmas dinner?"

"We usually go to our son's house for the holidays but my wife is bedridden now, so they visited us last weekend for an early Christmas gathering before heading off for a ski vacation in Colorado."

"Would you like a turkey?" As I unlocked the freezer door, I stopped to look at him. His facial expression clearly told me that he really hadn't expected much of anything

"To tell you the truth, I wouldn't know how to cook it, and I think it would be too much for us, but if you have a chicken, that would do," he said timidly.

I put the chicken in a separate bag then grabbed an apple pie and a box of chicken stuffing and put them in the bag with the fruits and vegetables. I added more groceries to get them through the week and put them in a cart.

"Come on. Let's get these into your car before they spoil." Trying not to let the thought of them being all alone on Christmas make me teary eyed, I busied myself with the task of unloading the groceries.

"I would like to volunteer sometime, perhaps when I don't have to stay home to care for my wife. Would you be able to use me here at the ministry?" He seemed genuinely interested.

"We'd love that, Mr. Hanson. Just come by when you are ready and we'll be glad to have your help. I will have someone call you next week to conduct an assessment to see how we can help in the interim. Please give your wife my best and take care." I gave him a hug.

His eyes filled with tears as he hugged me back and said, "Merry Christmas, and thank you!"

As I walked back to my office, I thought, "No, it's me who should be thanking you." In that moment I understood why I had felt the need to go in to the office that morning.

Chapter 25

Over the course of my career, I have learned a great deal about working with so many different populations. When serving the homeless, we are constantly reminded of how vulnerable this population is as they struggle to survive each day. Inevitably, people always ask me,

"What will it take to solve homelessness? Can we ever get people off the streets?"

I have learned over the years that you must meet people where they are, make the resources available to them and let them decide how far they wish to go.

A perfect example of this occurred many years ago when I found myself overseeing a small hunger relief organization in Houston's impoverished Fifth Ward. The morning food distribution was over and the lobby that had been teaming with seniors trying to make their social security checks stretch, families living hand to mouth, and near homeless folks just down on their luck, was now empty. Staff and volunteers were restocking the pantry, entering data, and returning phone calls. I was in my office when one of my employees, Michelle, came in.

"Carole, can you come out to the lobby? I'd like you to meet someone."

I followed Michelle to the lobby not knowing who or what to expect and as I got closer to the doorway, I saw a man in tattered clothing with his head down, he appeared to be sleeping. His hair was stringy and unkempt; his dark skinned arms were covered with insect bites that had become infected. They were swollen and looked very painful.

Michelle handed me a tube of cortisone for the bites. "I'll be right back with his food order."

The man was at least six-foot-five. His shoes were so worn out, they were wrapped with duct tape to hold them together. While I was used to the smell of unwashed bodies, having worked with the homeless population for many years, this was overpowering.

As I handed the gentleman the cream, I said, "I'm Carole. Michelle will be right back with your food. In the meantime I wanted to ask you where you have been staying."

He lifted his head slightly and glanced at me, "A friend has been letting me stay behind his shed." It was no wonder he was so eaten up. He was fair game to the mosquito population that was at an all-time high during an unusually hot August in the Bayou city.

"How long have you been sleeping outside?"

"A few months," he said with his eyes closed. No wonder he was exhausted. He hadn't had a full night of uninterrupted sleep in a long time. Michelle came back with a bag of food, which he gratefully accepted. "Do you mind if I eat while we talk?" he asked.

"Feel free," I said as I watched him tear open the loaf of bread and stuff it in his mouth, three and four slices at a time, crumbs falling everywhere.

"I'm sorry. It's been a while since I've eaten."

"Don't apologize," I said, wondering how this happens in our country in this day and age. "Are you interested in finding more permanent shelter?"

He did not glance up at me as he poured cereal into his mouth from an open box. "Sure," he replied in between gulps.

I went to get him some water to wash everything down and when I returned, he seemed to be eating at a more moderate pace. He drank the bottle of water in a few seconds and I handed him another. What could have happened to make a human being get to this level? I went over to the desk in the lobby and wrote down the address of a rooming house that charged by the week.

"If you decide to check this out, tell the manager, Greg, that Carole sent you. We will pay the first week directly to him. If you want to stay there, there are plenty of day labor jobs available. Just ask Greg."

Michelle came back with a shirt saying, "Unfortunately we don't have any pants or shoes in your size right now."

Our clothing donations were at an all-time low and went very quickly whenever we did get them in.

"If you come back in a few days, we'll have something set aside for you. What's your name?" I asked.

Wrapping up the bag of day old donuts, without looking up, he said, "Robert."

"Okay, then, Robert, you can use the bathroom to wash up if you like before you put the cream on your bites. I'll call Greg to let him know you are coming, and we'll see you in a few days."

As he headed toward the men's room, Michelle and I exchanged sorrowful glances, shaking our heads. Day in and day out we saw so many people down on their luck but this was such an extreme case. If Robert didn't get off the streets soon, he probably wouldn't survive much longer.

As I walked back to my office, I gave thanks for my warm bed, hot and cold running water, air conditioning, a more than adequate home, a loving family, good food, and access to healthcare. Why was I blessed with all these things, while others like Robert went without? What circumstances had led Robert to his current state of poverty? I went home that night and hugged my family a little more than usual.

Robert did come back a few days later and Michelle gave him the clothes she had set aside. But as the weeks passed, we figured he had moved on since Greg said he never showed up at the boarding house. I said a silent prayer for him and hoped he would survive.

Several months later, Michelle knocked on my door to my office. I was on the phone and motioned her to come in. She mouthed the words, "Someone is here to see you."

I held up one finger to let her know I'd be right there. As I got closer to the lobby, I could not see anyone sitting in the rows of chairs that lined the wall but as I turned the corner, I saw a tall man dressed in an expensive jogging suit. He was well groomed and rather handsome. His eyes lit up when he saw me as if he knew me.

"Ms. Carole, how are you?" He could tell by the blank look on my face that I did not remember him. "It's me, Robert," he said with a big smile while extending his hand to shake mine. "I just wanted to come by and say thank you before I left town." I couldn't believe my eyes. How could this be the same man? He gave me a hug and I hugged him back.

"I am so glad you did. We often wondered how you were doing. Look at you! You look fabulous. Thank you so much for coming by to see us. Is there anything we can do for you?"

His smile lit up his entire face as he said, "No, Ms. Carole. I'm in a better place now. I'm leaving Houston but didn't want to leave without saying thanks and to let you know what a little kindness will do for a person." I hugged him again because the lump in my throat wouldn't let me say anything else. I never heard from or saw Robert again but I hope he remains in a better place. I know my life is changed forever because of him.

Over the last thirteen years, I have learned so much from my staff, volunteers and donors about the true meaning of fellowship and community. I am now serving with a much larger coalition of congregations united in meeting the basic needs of the people in our area. Initially, I thought ministry was a religious activity meant for people of the cloth. I remember feeling fraudulent in my role as a ministry leader when I was first given the role. I didn't feel worthy. I have always believed that I must live my faith but never felt comfortable leading others in prayer, quoting the Bible, or for that matter, spontaneously praying anything other than the formal prayers I had been taught. The work has changed all that for me.

My daily work has taught me that ministry is the act of using your God given talents to help others. In my case, my responsibility has grown to finding ways to engage others in ministry. I believe we are all put here in this world to help one another; it is the best way to find your inner self. I don't believe we are here to amass wealth, power or fame, but we do have an obligation to be the best we can possibly be. Once I let go of worrying about how much money I made, I no longer struggled as I had in my youth. I now focus on doing what makes my heart sing. Whenever I find myself worrying about superficial things, something will happen to bring me back into focus. One of the most important things I learned from a member of my staff years ago is that "it's not always about you or what you want."

What I love about my work is that every day is filled with tiny miracles. As one problem presents itself, the solution magically appears. I still get goose bumps from time to time as I watch each day unfold. Back in 2001, Houston was hit hard by Tropical Storm Allison and much of Houston was under water for days. In the Port of Houston, a total of almost forty inches of rain was reported. The six-day rainfall in Houston flooded more than 95,000 cars and 73,000 homes throughout Harris County, leaving more than 30,000 homeless with residential damages totaling more than $1.75 billion. Several hospitals in the Texas Medical Center, the largest medical complex in the world, experienced severe damage from the storm's unexpected fury. Many people could not leave their homes or their subdivisions until the water receded.

It was three days before I could make my way to the ministry because so many roads were unsurpassable. While many neighborhoods were still under water after the rain stopped, our little ministry was high and dry, and when I opened the door of the lobby, I was amazed at all the donations of food, blankets, clothing, water, and gifts of love that had been donated by area residents who knew that in times of need, people arrived on our doorstep. It was as though angels had descended upon us, and just when I began to wonder how I was going to manage and distribute all these gifts in addition to operating our regular programs and services, groups of volunteers began to arrive and the phones began to ring.

Allison was the training exercise for what was to follow in 2005, because when Katrina hit New Orleans, more than 200,000 stranded Louisianans found their way to Houston. Even though our social service ministry is located more than twenty-five miles from the Astrodome, we served over 15,000 individuals whose lives had been changed forever. This was a disaster that no one could have prepared for, yet once again donations and volunteers arrived daily to minister to the shell shocked evacuees. No one was turned away and we never ran out of donations.

The ministry has taught me so much about who I am, why I am here, and most of all to accept what comes my way. If things become difficult and I have truly given it my all, then I must be open to other possibilities.

One day I pulled up to the front of the ministry a little after six thirty in the morning. I had a long list of things to accomplish before staff arrived and wanted to get a jump start. As I got out of the car, I noticed an older model van in the parking lot but could not see who was behind the wheel. I entered the building, turned off the alarm and as I headed back toward my car to park it in the rear parking area, I could now see a middle aged woman in the driver's seat. Since it would be a few hours before programs started seeing people, I decided to see what she needed.

She smiled as I approached her. "I know I'm here early but I had to drop my husband off at his day labor job and don't have enough gas to go home and come back. I thought it would be best to just wait."

As the Houston sun beat down and the day began to heat up, I noticed she already had beads of sweat forming on her brow as she continued,

"We've had a rough time of it lately because my husband was a long-distance truck driver and the long hours and time away from home were really affecting his health. It was hard on me and the kids, too, so he decided to drive locally. But it doesn't pay as well and the work isn't steady. I came here today to see about getting some professional clothing so that I can look for a job. My dream is to help troubled youth, and I volunteer at my church helping as much as I can, but the pastor says times are tough. As much as he would like to hire me, there's not enough money in the budget."

I could see the tears beginning to well up as she spoke of her desire to do well in the world.

"I know God has a plan for us, it's just a little tough right now. I am trying to stay strong for my family."

I placed my hand on her shoulder and said, "If you stay focused and don't give up, you'll get there. I'll be right back."

I thought about her struggles and remembering my own, knew how important it was to have hope. I returned a few minutes later with a few gift cards to help her with gas, groceries and clothing.

"This isn't much but it will help get you started on your journey."

She accepted the cards, tears freely flowing now, "I prayed for direction this morning and He sent me here. Bless you."

If she only knew how blessed I was already in that moment. We prayed together for a minute and spontaneously hugged one another. As I walked away, my heart was full and turning back toward her, I promised, "Remember, you are never alone."

She waived and smiled as she pulled out of the parking lot.

Chapter 26

It was an initial surprise to hear my mother's voice on my cell phone that day over a year ago. At first I thought maybe she was kidding when she said she needed desktop support, so I said,

"Excuse me?" with a small glimmer of hope that things would be right again between us, that she would do and say all the things that daughters want their mothers to do and say.

Once again she explained,

"I'm having problems with my computer and I need desktop support."

Listening to my mother repeat her request for desktop support, I recalled it had been almost four years since I had last spoken to her. The conversation the last time she called was around my brother Bob, who had come to live with us six months prior. Bob had called me out of the blue in the summer of 2006 to let me know he had been thinking about me and wanted to see how I was doing. It was the first time my brother had ever called me since I left my mother's house at the age of twelve.

More than twenty-five years prior, I had reached out to all my mother's kids with an offer to pay for college if they wanted to come and live with me. Surprisingly, they were not interested and seemed content with the lives they were living.

We spoke for a while and it was evident that Bob was not doing well. He was in a rut and very depressed. The more we talked, the more my heart went out to my younger brother. After I left all those years ago, Bob became the oldest of five and the chief line of defense between my younger brothers and sisters in the dysfunctional world they had been exposed to by my mother and the men in her life.

Bob sounded like he was at the end of his rope, "I have nothing to look forward to here. I got so sick and tired of all the garbage at work. I just couldn't take it anymore so I gave my notice."

Always in the survival mode, I asked,

"Do you have anything lined up?"

"Yeah, Jimmy and his wife, Hope, have a few group homes. They said they'd hire me if I was interested."

Jimmy, our youngest half-brother, who is the spitting image of Paul, was married with two little girls and seemed to be doing okay.

Trying to sound supportive I said,

"Well that sounds good. What do you think?"

"Hope is hard to get along with. She's nice enough at first, but she gets pretty demanding. I don't know if I can put up with it too long, and since it's family, it'll get messy."

"Any other options?" I wondered how I could help or if he would even accept my help.

"I don't know. I'm so fed up with everything. This apartment sucks but it's all I can afford on my own. The kids are all screwed up, they don't listen to me. I don't even want to go see them anymore. The only one I feel sorry for is Danny, Beth's boy. But I can't help him either because I can't even help myself."

Bob desperately needed a change of pace so I purchased a plane ticket and arranged for transportation to Logan Airport in Boston so that he could come for a visit and get to know his niece, nephew, and brother-in-law whom he had never met. It felt good to be able to do something to help my brother. I was excited to have the kids meet one of their uncles for the first time. Up until now, my kids only had a relationship with my husband's side of the family. I couldn't wait to share my life with my brother after all these years.

When I met Bob at the airport, he looked haggard and unkempt. Upon seeing me, his eyes lit up, and when I looked at his face, I saw the little brother I had once cared for. He knew more about me and the life we had shared so long ago than my husband and children. Our few days together melted the time and distance of all the lost years. It was like finding my way back home. Bob validated my childhood memories of the rocky life spent with our mother and her love interests, and I filled in the gaps for the times he was too young to remember. My heart broke when I listened to how he became the principal caretaker after I left. Our time together flew, and I had tears in my eyes when I dropped him off at the airport after our week together. It was then that I offered my heart and my home to my brother should he ever need me. A few weeks later, Bob took me up on my offer. He said he needed help to climb out of the rut he was in. Without even consulting with my husband or my kids, I sent Bob the ticket. I couldn't wait to provide the tools that Bob would need to create the life he wanted.

Bob moved into our daughter's room, and she moved into our room. The plan was to get Bob job-ready, so we spent the next several days buying interview clothes and accessories beyond the jeans and t-shirts he had brought with him from Massachusetts. We made a stop at the local barber shop then went shopping for a cell phone. My husband worked with Bob to create a resume and taught him how to navigate the Internet and email so that he could begin his job search in earnest. I introduced Bob to the short-term certificate and degree programs offered by the local community college, but he seemed uninterested.

"I want to focus on getting a job first," he said.

My husband and I drove Bob to various retail outlets so he could apply in person, and when he wasn't job searching, he helped out with meals and household chores. It was great having another adult to be there when the kids got home. After a few months, Bob's enthusiasm for the job search began to wane as he had only been called for one job that paid $6.50 per hour and was part-time from eleven p.m. to seven a.m., which Bob promptly turned down. I couldn't believe my ears.

"Did I just hear you tell that woman you weren't interested?"

Bob popped open a beer, "I didn't come all the way to Texas to earn less than what I was earning in Massachusetts."

"Bob, you were unemployed in Massachusetts."

"You know what I mean. I was making $10 an hour at my last job. I at least want to start at that level." He clicked on the remote as he reclined in the chair to watch football.

"The cost of living is lower here, Bob. With a high school diploma and your experience, the most you can expect to start at is $8.50 if you get a job as a mental health aide. Right now, until you can get your foot in the door, you need to take whatever comes your way in the retail sector."

"I hear you, but I'm not taking a job that has me working nights and weekends earning $6.50 an hour. I want my weekends free to watch the games."

My antennae went up. The games? My forty-six-year-old, unemployed, beer-drinking brother who was down to his last hundred dollars said, "Yeah, I like to keep my weekends free to watch the games." Bob had over a thousand dollars with him when he arrived. We told him to keep that for a rainy day, and we picked up the tab from that day forward. Later we learned Bob spent all his savings on beer and Jack Daniel's bourbon during that time.

Bob took a job working the night crew at Wal-Mart then eventually found a job as a mental health aide at an adult day care facility about ten miles from the house. They offered him a higher paying position that required living in the residential side of the facility Thursday night through Sunday or a lower paying position that was eight to five Monday through Friday. I tried to encourage Bob to see the advantages of the higher paying position. He wouldn't need a car to go back and forth every day. We could drop him off and pick him up just as we were doing now. It would allow him to either go to school the rest of the week or keep his job at Wal-Mart until he saved up enough to go out on his own. Bob chose the lower paying job.

Since Bob's new job was located forty miles in the complete opposite direction from my office and Keith's schedule changed weekly, we decided the best thing to do was to help Bob buy a car. Keith took Bob car shopping and in a few hours, Bob was pulling into the drive way behind the wheel of a brand new car. It warmed my heart to see that Keith had gone the extra mile to help my brother and put the note in his name. Bob agreed to pay the insurance and car payments each month.

The next day, I took Bob shopping and bought a few more outfits for work. The weeks went by and Bob seemed to be adjusting well at work. He talked about how he was making a good impression by treating the clients with dignity and respect. The clients were already asking for him by name if Bob wasn't waiting to help them off the bus when they arrived. Bob appeared happy and after a while began to go out with coworkers after work. On the weekends, he played softball with his boss and several other people from the facility.

The months began to pass, and Bob's drinking seemed to become more intense. He no longer helped out around the house. He would sit in the living room in front of the television and drink one beer right after another. On the weekends, he drank so much that he would weave back and forth when he stood up. His speech was slurred and often unintelligible to the kids. I told Bob this was not the example we wanted him to set for our kids. Bob said he understood, and he would make sure it didn't happen again. He spent less time with the family and most of his time in his room with the door closed or out with friends.

One Friday night, my husband and I were watching a movie in the living room, and Bob came home close to midnight. As he stood there talking to us, it was apparent that he was in no condition to get behind the wheel of a car, and yet he had driven himself home that night. The next morning, we decided to have a talk with Bob about how he swore he would never drink and drive. He admitted to drinking way more than the legal limit and agreed with us that it was unacceptable. He said he would not do it again, but his promise was short-lived.

My very patient husband had reached the end of his rope and frankly, I could not blame him. He reminded me that I had brought my brother into the house without even consulting with him and that he had been very understanding and accepting. He could not however continue to live with Bob's drinking problem. It was not what he signed up for. The car was in his name, and he did not want to be responsible for Bob's actions. With a heavy heart, I knew he was right and after almost seven months of watching the situation deteriorate, it was time to confront Bob and give him an ultimatum.

Around mid-morning, when Bob finally came downstairs we asked him to join us outside on the back patio so the kids wouldn't hear.

"Bob, this was the hardest conversation I've ever had with anyone. Do you remember what you told me when you decided to move here?"

Bob nodded but didn't say anything.

"I thought I heard you say you wanted a chance to get ahead, to make a better life for yourself. Am I recalling correctly?"

"Yeah."

"We talked about what that meant, do you remember?"

Bob didn't move.

"You wanted to get a decent job, maybe go back to school and you wanted to save enough to live on your own, right? So how much do you have in the bank, now?"

"Counting my paycheck from this week, about $250," Bob fidgeted with the lose tile on the patio table.

"What happened to the thousand dollars you brought with you?"

"Well, that's gone," he shrugged, "I used it while I was looking for work."

"So what you're saying is, after seven months of us providing room, board, clothing, and whatever else you needed, you have nothing to show for it?"

"Well, I have to pay the car note and the insurance so it's hard to save anything."

"What's your take home, Bob?"

"About $265 a week."

"Your car note and insurance are around $320 a month, Bob. That leaves a little over $700 a month for savings and you've been working for almost five months. On the flip side, if you were paying rent, utilities and groceries for the last seven months, you would have spent over $5000 for a place half as nice as what you have here."

Bob sat quietly, staring at the table. Keith said, "Bob, a few weeks ago we spoke to you about drinking and driving. We all agreed that there would be no more of that. Besides the fact that you could hurt yourself and others, the car is in my name, and I do not want to be liable for your poor judgment."

"I'm sorry, Keith."

Bob looked genuinely apologetic, making it even harder for me to continue.

"Bob, it's obvious you have a problem that is getting in the way of what you want to accomplish. The way we see it, you have two choices. You can get help or you can move out on your own."

Bob looked at both of us and said,

"Okay." He stood up and walked back in to the house. We did not see him for the rest of the day. The next day, Bob left the house to go off to a softball game and never came back. A few days later we found out he decided to go back to Massachusetts.

While cleaning the bedroom Bob had been using, we discovered where most of Bob's money had gone. On the table next to Bob's bed was an empty 1.75-liter bottle of Jack Daniel's that Bob threw his spare change in to. The suitcase under the bed was filled with empty Jack Daniel's bottles of all sizes and the cabinets in the bathroom contained several dozen empty beer bottles. When we retrieved the car from the motel where Bob had been staying until he arranged his flight back to Massachusetts, we counted more than twenty Jack Daniel's bottles and scores of empty beer bottles in the trunk of the car.

In addition to the sadness I felt over not being able to help my brother, I mourned the loss of all communication with the maternal side of my family, who made it clear that my brother did not have a problem and that I owed it to him to take care of him.

As I stood in my office with the phone to my ear, contemplating my response to my mother, I thought how ironic that she would accidentally call me instead of Microsoft. I realized in that moment that she had my number on her speed dial. Her lack of contact with her grandchildren was a conscious choice and given all the baggage, it was for the better. Why was I continually hoping for a mother-daughter relationship that just was not possible? It was time for me to stop having false expectations.

Although things started out rocky for me, I was shooting for a much smoother ending. It was time to cut the emotional strings of longing for something my mother wasn't capable of giving.

I responded, "I'm sorry. You have the wrong number," and I felt an enormous weight lifted from my shoulders. I am now free to accept my family on my terms, not theirs.

Epilogue
2012

People would always tell me, "You should write a book." I guess it is most likely because I enjoy storytelling so much and find adventure in everyday life. Up until now, I never seriously entertained the idea because I didn't think anyone would be interested in reading about my life. All that changed last year when I met Jeannette Walls, author of *The Glass Castle*. After talking at length, I realized she wrote the book for herself. At the conclusion of our time together, Jeannette convinced me by saying, "Carole, you have a book in you and you need to tell your story."

Jeannette's words made me realize it was time to take a long, hard look at where I had come from and where I had been, in order to make peace with myself. The added bonus would come if it somehow could provide hope to those who find themselves in a negative environment or if it inspires others to take action to help those less fortunate.

While business writing is part of my everyday life, writing a memoir was totally unfamiliar territory to me and frankly, I didn't know where to start. After researching the process for several months and contacting a few writing coaches, I began working with Max Regan of Hollowdeck Press in Boulder, Colorado. Max helped me to understand the nuances of memoir and artfully guided me through this very personal and at times, very painful process of reliving the past. Wounds that I thought had long since healed, were once again pried open and laid bare. But the difference between now and then is that the healing lies in understanding my purpose in this life.

The wonderful thing about memoir is that it also helps you remember those who were instrumental in helping you get to the next level in a very meaningful way. In my case, I felt compelled to find them and thank them for the role they played and how much of a difference they made in my life.

The very first person I contacted was Bishop George Rueger, who at the age of eighty-two in the summer of 2011 was retired and still living in Worcester. I sent the bishop a note to thank him for bestowing such kindness on me when I appeared before him as a scared teenager back in the early 1970's. I was fearful that I would not be able to graduate from the private school I had been attending because I had "cut the strings" with my family, and they were no longer going to support me. While I was almost certain Bishop Rueger would not remember me, it was important for me to thank him. I wanted him to know that as he looked back over his life, he should feel proud that the kindness and generosity he showed me in my hour of need was something I tried to convey to those I meet every day through my work and daily life. I needed him to know that his legacy will live on, long after he leaves this earth.

I never expected to hear back and was taken by surprise when a letter appeared in my mailbox with a familiar return address. The enclosed note read:

"Carole,
Thank you – your note meant so much. I called Leo
Gravel, Miss O'Hearn. I am - we are proud of your
work. There is so much pain, poverty. We need your
ministry. All God's love. Keep it up.

Blessings galore,
Bishop"

The note was accompanied by another check for $100 in support of the ministry. I am overcome with emotion every time I read it. It is a written affirmation that my life is on the right path and that I am doing what I was meant to be doing. To think that the Bishop supported me then and he supports me now, even though more than thirty-five years have passed since we have seen one another. I think of all the students he knew as headmaster and all the people he has known during his life time as a priest and a bishop and remain in awe that he not only remembered me, he still believes in me.

While Mr. and Mrs. McGrail have passed away, I was able to make contact with Trisha McGrail, who unselfishly asked her parents to take me in when I didn't know where else to go. I had the good fortune to catch up with Trish and her sister Teresa, both of whom embraced me and gave me a place to call home. More importantly, they treated me as a family member, and I never felt that I did not belong. After spending a few days with Teresa last summer, it felt as though no time had passed between us, and we were family once again. I cried the day she left.

I have not been so successful in finding those with whom I lived and worked overseas. I read accounts of the Hmong people, many of whom have been in the United States for more than thirty years, and still continue to struggle with cultural, religious and racial differences. I have been in touch with former coworkers like Lucinda Rice, who was a port in a storm when I needed one most at the time of my son's birth. It is such a joyful experience to be able to say thank you to those who made such a difference in my life. Each time I make contact with someone from my past, they are genuinely surprised that their actions meant so much and are truly touched by my gratitude.

On a sad note, I continue to be estranged from the maternal side of my family, and this point was driven home when I was recently informed that my maternal grandmother had passed away. I received an email from my stepmother with a link to the obituary which listed me and my children. None of my siblings or my mother ever contacted me. While painful, I accept this as the down side to "cutting the strings" in order to live the life I was meant to live. It has become an all-too-familiar side of my life, which many do not understand. The only ones who do understand are those who have made the painful choice to move forward and leave the negative influences behind. Since writing the book,

I continually meet people who are on the verge of making a change but remain fearful of the unknown. I meet still others that have made the leap and talk of how free they feel because they are no longer held back.

My dad and stepmother have visited many times over the last few decades, and I have made the trip back to New England on several occasions as well. While I initially hoped to be close to my dad's children once again, they don't remember me ever living with them, and it is clear they do not really see me as a sibling. I am grateful, however, for any contact when it does occur so that my own children will have an extended family.

There are pros and cons to everything in life and while cutting the strings was painfully lonely until I had a family to call my own, I have no regrets. I am living the life I dreamed of with a loving and supportive family, meaningful work, and good friends.

In 2007, the same year my first-born entered college, I decided to finish what I had started almost thirty years ago. I went on to get my master's degree and at fifty-four years old, graduated with my husband who decided to follow my lead.

I read somewhere that when you examine your life, it is usually the most painful experiences that lead you to ministry. I have been fortunate in so many ways and will continue to live my life paying it forward so that others may benefit from the kindnesses bestowed upon me.

Whenever I feel stuck, I continually ask myself, what I am I willing to give up in order to get to where I want to be. For me, cutting the strings brought many challenges along with many rewards.

Website References

The End of the Hmong
www.paulbogdanor.com/left/laos.html

Ban Vinai
www.parkridgecenter.org/Page457.html

Refugee Medicine in Thailand
www.ncbi.nlm.nih.gov/pmc/articles/PMC22795
22/pdf/tacca00097-0103.pdf

15294736R00112

Made in the USA
Charleston, SC
27 October 2012